To Save a Starfish

To Save a Starfish

**A COMPASSION-FATIGUE WORKBOOK FOR
THE ANIMAL-WELFARE WARRIOR**

Jennifer A. Blough, LLPC

ISBN-13: 9780692755426
ISBN-10: 069275542X
Library of Congress Control Number: 2016911405
Jennifer Blough, New Boston, MI

In memory of Albert.

Disclaimer from the Author

This workbook is intended to help you develop an understanding of compassion fatigue and recognize how it may impact you personally and professionally. It is not meant to provide medical advice or substitute for psychological care. Please consult with a mental-health professional if you feel that you may be suffering from depression, anxiety, or posttraumatic stress disorder. If you feel suicidal, go to your nearest emergency room or contact 911 immediately. Please note that while I have tried to keep graphic details to a minimum, certain content in this workbook may be upsetting to some readers.

Contents

Acknowledgments

Thank you to my family and friends for your love and support. Thank you to my grandma for opening my eyes to animal welfare. A special thank you to my husband—you not only supported this lifestyle, but you also embraced it; I will never be able to put into words how grateful I am. Thanks to all those quoted throughout this book who were willing to share their stories with me. Thanks to Vicki Brett-Gach for your wonderful contribution to the nutrition section. And thank you to my rock-star team of beta readers: Dr. Amanda Charney, Kate Christlieb, Allen Larsen, Jay Mallonee, Kelly Morton, Maureen O'Nell, and Brad Shear.

The Starfish Story

An old man was walking along the beach when he noticed a young woman off in the distance. As he got closer, he noticed that the woman was collecting starfish that had washed up on the beach and tossing them, one by one, back into the ocean. "Excuse me, young lady, but what are you doing?" the old man asked.

"All these starfish have been washed up by the tide. If I don't throw them back, they will die," she replied.

"But there are hundreds and hundreds of starfish on the beach," the old man said. "You can't possibly make a difference."

The young woman listened politely, bent down, picked up another starfish, and tossed it into the ocean. She looked at the old man and replied, "It made a difference for that one."

Adapted from "The Star Thrower," by Loren Eisely

Part One

CHAPTER 1

Introduction: What is Compassion Fatigue?

I care so much it hurts sometimes.
−Dr. Bev Heater, Veterinarian, Maryland

have been involved in animal welfare for as long as I can remember. I'm pretty sure it all started when, as a young child, I learned that hamburger was a code word for cow. Little did I know that my refusal to eat meat was just the beginning of what would become a lifelong dedication to helping animals in need. As a young adult, I became involved in animal rescue and have since volunteered and worked with various animal welfare organizations. I've scooped poop, and I've cleaned kennels. I've been a foster parent and a euthanasia technician. I've worn both the boots and the sandals—meaning that I've worked on the law-enforcement side and the shelter side. I've burned out, and I've bounced back. I've seen the worst in people, and I've met some of the most kind-hearted and selfless people on the planet.

My role in animal welfare—and my life—took a turn when my little feathered soul mate, Albert, died suddenly. The devastation and grief that I felt were indescribable, and those feelings took me to a very dark place. When I finally emerged, I decided to go back to graduate school to study psychology. I wanted to honor Albert by helping others who had lost their own pets. I also wanted to help all the animal-welfare warriors out there who dedicate their lives to caring for animals and who struggle with the pain that sometimes comes with this unique, rewarding, and challenging career and/or lifestyle.

I've personally felt frustration and even anger toward the public as they've lined up at the local shelter with boxes of unwanted puppies and kittens, stray dogs and cats, hamsters the kids stopped caring for, and parrots who either were too loud or didn't talk. I've been filled with disgust by the sight of dogs covered in scars—physical and emotional—from years of fighting, farm animals too sick and emaciated to even stand, and cats who have been mutilated for someone's idea of sick, twisted fun. I've felt my lungs burning from the stench of ammonia inside hoarders' homes. I've felt the guilt, heartache, and rage that came with giving that fatal dose of "blue juice" to all the animals I couldn't save. For those of you who work, volunteer, or are in any way involved in animal welfare, you may have had similar experiences—or at least similar feelings—in response to the harsh realities of the field. The reality of pet overpopulation, animal abuse, dog fighting, factory farming—the list goes on—can take a hefty toll on those of us who care the most. In fact, research has shown that those of us who have high levels of empathy, which is the ability to *literally* feel another's pain and suffering, are at a greater risk of developing compassion fatigue (Figley 2012).

So What is Compassion Fatigue Anyway?

Compassion fatigue has been described by traumatologist Charles Figley (1982) as the "cost of caring for others in emotional pain." In his book *Compassion Fatigue: Coping with Secondary Traumatic Stress Disorder in Those Who Treat the Traumatized* (1995), he adds that "the display of symptoms is the natural consequence of stress resulting from caring for and helping traumatized or suffering people or animals." In other words, whether you're a humane officer or a shelter volunteer, a vet tech or an animal-rights activist, you have likely seen, heard about, or experienced things that most people can't even begin to understand. Long-term exposure to abuse and neglect, trauma, euthanasia, grief-stricken clients, etc., can not only impact your work productivity and satisfaction, but it can also wear on you mentally, physically, emotionally, and spiritually. If you don't learn to manage the stress associated with helping others, then your compassion satisfaction can slowly fade, leaving you feeling angry, depressed, anxious, physically exhausted, and emotionally drained. Compassion fatigue can affect your professional life and spill over into your personal life. Eventually, it may even lead to burnout, which causes some people to leave the field altogether.

Does this mean that if you choose to devote yourself to helping animals then you're destined to a life of suffering? Absolutely not. One of the most important advancements in animal welfare, in my opinion, is the acknowledgment that compassion fatigue exists. It's a common topic of discussion in other helping fields like nursing, social work, and counseling. And although it may sometimes seem like animal welfare is the "red-headed stepchild" of the helping professions, the good news is that we've begun to recognize it. When I started in the field, we didn't talk about it. I didn't even know there was a name for what I was going through. This needs to change because many of you are crashing and burning. Did you know that animal-control officers have the highest suicide rate—along with police officers and firefighters—of all workers in the United States? (Tiesman et al. 2015). In fact, recent research revealed that an alarming one in six veterinarians in the United States has considered suicide (Larkin 2015). Another study revealed that veterinarians in the United Kingdom have a suicide rate of an astonishing four times the general population (Tremayne 2010). Folks, we have *got* to start talking about this!

So what is the antidote to compassion fatigue? Currently, what we know is that it is a combination of self-care (something helping professionals can often struggle with) and support. Let's take the former—what does that look like? Think of it as a way to recharge your battery. People I've met and worked with in the animal welfare field often feel guilty or even selfish when taking time for themselves, and I've felt that way too. I'll admit it took me a long time to realize that if I didn't take care of myself, then I couldn't take care of the animals very well either.

Whether you are new to the animal welfare community or a seasoned veteran, this workbook is designed to help you recognize the symptoms and warning signs so that you can take steps to prevent, manage, or overcome compassion fatigue. This workbook was created for shelter workers and volunteers, animal-control officers, veterinary staff, rescue workers, trainers and behaviorists, wildlife rehabilitators, humane investigators, animal attorneys, foster parents, ethical vegetarians and vegans, animal-rights activists, pet sitters, dog walkers, groomers, and (of course) all-around animal lovers. For all you animal-welfare warriors out there, whether you are behind the scenes or on the front lines fighting to protect innocent animals, this book is dedicated to you.

As someone who has worked in the trenches, it is my hope that I can now offer what you may need the most—compassion, validation, and understanding, along with some ammunition to help you continue to wage this seemingly endless battle. For every one we save, there are countless others who need us. And sometimes the best way to help is to help ourselves.

This workbook provides many practical and proven strategies to help you reduce anxiety, let go of anger, ward off depression, manage stress, and improve your overall well-being. Not only will you discover techniques for conquering compassion fatigue, but you'll also learn how to cultivate compassion satisfaction—the key to staying strong, healthy, and energized so that you can continue to fight for those who don't have a voice.

How to Get the Most from this Workbook

You may find that certain sections or chapters of this workbook really hit home for you or that some of the self-care tools might appeal to you more than others. Your journey to combat compassion fatigue—and through this workbook—is a very personal one and should be honored as such. While I do encourage you to read the entire book from cover to cover for maximum benefit, feel free to skip to the parts that interest you the most. When you get to the tools chapter, however, I strongly suggest that you learn the art of mindful deep breathing first, as that's an important component to some of the other techniques throughout the book.

This workbook is divided into three parts, each ending with a story that chronicles the struggles and successes of a fellow animal-welfare warrior. It is my hope that these personal stories provide inspiration and serve as a reminder of the importance of the incredible work that you do. After you complete the workbook, you'll notice that the last story is blank; I encourage you to use this space to reflect on your own trials and tribulations, as well as your triumphs, and write your own starfish story.

So, for now, take a deep breath and enjoy the journey!

CHAPTER 2

The Consequences of Caring

I've had recurring nightmares about animals needing me...I dream that I am standing between two conveyor belts and kittens are coming toward me. I have to pick the kittens up off one belt and place them on the other belt to send them to a safe place. My arms are exhausted, but I know that if I stop, the kittens will fall into the pit below. So I keep going.
—HANNAH SHAW, ANIMAL ADVOCATE AND RESCUE WORKER, WASHINGTON, DC

From the moment Kate Dubuque wakes up, her work begins. On a typical day, she's answered phone calls, responded to e-mails, cleaned kennels, bathed dogs, arranged for veterinary care, found foster homes, met with potential adopters—and all before lunchtime, too. Dubuque, a vet tech, is the founder of Little Rhody Rescue and Quarantine, a small animal-rescue facility in Rhode Island. To date, the organization has been responsible for placing close to nine thousand dogs into loving homes. Yet, despite this accomplishment, Dubuque often feels overwhelmed by the sheer number of animals in need. "I don't necessarily feel like a failure, but I wish I had more help and the capacity to do more," she says. "That tendency to wish you could do more is always there...the reality that no matter what you do, there will always be more." Not only is there always more, but there is never enough. Never enough money, never enough time, and never enough homes. This harsh reality often leaves Dubuque feeling physically and emotionally exhausted and plagued with the thought, "Maybe you're not smart enough, capable enough, strong enough…maybe *you're* not enough."

Is Compassion Fatigue the Same as Burnout?

The too-much-and-not-enough dilemma is common to animal rescuers around the globe, and it can play a major role in the development of both compassion fatigue and professional burnout. And while they share many similarities and can coexist, compassion fatigue and burnout have some notable differences. According to Patricia Smith, burnout, unlike compassion fatigue, is a process that can slowly creep up on anyone, regardless of his or her profession. The founder of the Compassion Fatigue Awareness Project adds that burnout results from "not enough—not enough time, not enough resources, not enough energy" (Dolce 2013). Compassion fatigue, on the other hand, tends to occur more quickly and is unique to those who work with suffering or traumatized populations. Throw in some stress, which Smith describes as "too much—too much work, too much pressure, too many deadlines" (Dolce 2013), and you're left feeling damaged by this perfect storm.

Could I Be Suffering from Compassion Fatigue?

Before we talk about how it develops and who may be at risk, let's take a look at some of the symptoms associated with compassion fatigue. Now, if you are like many others in the helping professions, then you probably tend to put the needs of others before your own. But I encourage you to take a few moments to get in touch with where you are right now. Below are some of the symptoms that people with compassion fatigue may display, and they may resonate with you:

- **Depression or Feelings of Sadness:** Everyone gets the blues from time to time. But when feelings of sadness become chronic, then this can indicate compassion fatigue or possibly even depression. Depression can make you feel like the life is being sucked out of you. It may be difficult to get out of bed in the morning, and you may feel like you're dragging yourself around all day. Negativity and apathy are also common—you may feel as if there's no point to anything.

- **Insomnia or Hypersomnia:** While many of us experience occasional trouble falling or staying asleep, insomnia can become downright debilitating when we experience it night after sleepless night. Hypersomnia, which is the tendency to sleep too much, can also have a negative impact on our personal and professional lives. Both might be a sign of compassion fatigue.

- **Flashbacks and/or Nightmares:** Sometimes disturbing images of the things we've witnessed can haunt our dreams and even creep up on us during our waking hours. These intrusive thoughts cause great distress and can be symptomatic of compassion fatigue, but they are also common in those suffering from posttraumatic stress disorder (PTSD).

- **Fatigue or Low Energy:** Animal-welfare work, which often seems like an uphill battle, can be downright exhausting. Combine the emotionally charged nature of the work with a lack of self-care and you'll end up feeling drained.

- **Anger or Irritability:** This symptom used to be a personal favorite of mine. People in the animal-welfare community can sometimes become jaded by what they experience day in and day out. Add to that the often-ignorant and difficult general public with their lack of understanding, and you're bound to become angry or irritable.

- **Grief:** We may not necessarily associate this symptom with animal-welfare work. But, if you think about it, some of you witness or hear about death on a daily basis. Whether you perform euthanasia or fight factory farming, grief is a normal reaction to the inevitable losses we so often face.

- **Withdrawal:** Who has the energy to be social after a long day of giving 110 percent of yourself to your work? Not to mention, who can you talk to who will actually understand what you're going through? When compassion fatigue takes over, it's common to want to go home, curl up in a ball in front of the TV, and zone out.

- **Feelings of Isolation:** Given society's view on animals, it's no surprise that our beliefs and the work that we do can make us feel isolated. Euthanasia, for example, is not exactly an appropriate topic for the dinner table. Outside of the animal-welfare community, it may be difficult for you to find others who can support—let alone understand—your cause, which can understandably lead to your feeling lonely or disconnected from friends, family, and even the world.

- **Appetite Changes:** Perhaps you've lost your appetite—or the opposite extreme—you turn to food for comfort. If you're stress eating or not eating much at all, then it may be that you have too much on your plate, so to speak.

- **Loss of Interest:** A loss of interest or feeling of apathy can be a common symptom of both compassion fatigue and depression. You may find that activities you once enjoyed no longer bring you pleasure; instead, you walk around feeling, well, just sort of blah.

- **Feelings of Guilt:** Animal-welfare workers tend to carry the weight of the world on their shoulders. We really do put unrealistic and unfair expectations upon ourselves, and when we realize that we can't save them all, we may feel like a failure. Feelings of guilt are sure to surface when we don't accept our own limitations.

- **Lack of Motivation:** A life devoted to animal welfare can be overwhelming at times. In fact, we might feel so overwhelmed that we become paralyzed. We might feel hopeless or that the work we do is pointless, and so we may think, "Why even bother anymore?"

- **Relationship Conflicts:** Compassion fatigue can drain us to the point where we find it difficult to get along with others. Conflict can creep up between you and your intimate partner, family and friends, coworkers and colleagues, and even clients and customers.

- **Feelings of Emptiness:** Sometimes we work so hard to give to others that we have nothing left to give ourselves. We give and give to the point of depletion.

- **Work Issues:** Maybe you've noticed that you've started to cut corners or are habitually late to work. Whether you've been calling in sick more than usual or simply find yourself not as productive while on the clock, compassion fatigue can rear its ugly head on the job.

- **Feeling Numb, Like a Zombie:** Do you ever feel like you're just going through the motions? If you find yourself on auto-pilot most of the time, zoned out, or less compassionate and caring than you used to be, chances are you've got a fairly high level of compassion fatigue.

- **Anxiety:** Anxiety can manifest itself in several ways, mentally and physically. Perhaps you find yourself worrying all the time or often feel "on edge." Or maybe you've noticed that your breathing is shallow or that your heart is beating fast. If so, listen to your body—it's trying to tell you something.

- **Low Self-Esteem:** Sometimes our sense of self is based on the work we do for others. For example, when we adopt out that special animal or perform life-saving surgery, we feel good about ourselves. But when we lose that animal abuse case or have to put an animal down, our self-esteem sometimes tanks.

- **Poor Concentration:** Like physical exhaustion, mental fatigue is a common symptom of compassion fatigue. When chronic stress is combined with a lack of proper self-care, including poor nutrition and sleep, brain fog can result, affecting our judgment and making it difficult to focus and make decisions.

- **Bodily Complaints:** Do you suffer with daily headaches, stomach pains, or tight muscles? Have you been getting sick more often than usual? While it's important to have your doctor rule out any possible medical causes, these physical ailments could also be signs of compassion fatigue.

- **Feeling "On Guard":** Just like emergency-room doctors or firefighters, some of you often work through situations that involve life and death. Because of this, you have probably trained yourself to be ready to respond at the drop of a hat. But being in a constant state of hypervigilance, especially when you're off the clock, can cause a lot of health problems, both physical and mental.

- **Unhealthy Coping Skills:** We all need a vice, but when compassion fatigue sets in, we sometimes turn to unhealthy coping skills like using drugs or drinking alcohol, binge eating, impulsive shopping, or having unsafe sex. While they may seem to help in the moment, these risky behaviors are really just Band-Aids that only hurt us in the long run.

- **Negative Worldview:** It can be difficult for us to appreciate the positive things in life when we're exposed to so much suffering. Our whole outlook may change or we may start to feel hopeless about the future.

- **Suicidal Thoughts:** Have you ever felt so overwhelmed or hopeless that you believed that suicide was the only way out? If you're consumed with thoughts of death and dying, then you may be suffering from a severe form of compassion fatigue or depression. Please know that help is available! It is imperative that you find a mental-health professional to help you cope with the deep pain you are feeling.

If any of the above symptoms sound all-too-familiar, then you may be suffering from compassion fatigue. If so, I want to congratulate you on having the strength and the wisdom to pick up this book—you just may have taken the first step toward recovery. This is not to say that compassion fatigue is an illness or mental disorder. It's imperative that you remember that you are *not* weak, sick, or crazy and, most importantly, that you are *not* alone. Compassion fatigue is simply the consequence of caring for others, and it's also common to a variety of other helping professionals, including police officers, firefighters, nurses, paramedics, and even therapists. In fact, traumatologist Eric Gentry has suggested that those of us who are drawn to helping others may actually suffer from compassion fatigue to some degree *before* we even enter the field (The Compassion Fatigue Awareness Project 2013). How can this be? Let's take a look at some of the factors that may contribute to compassion fatigue.

Personality and Temperament

If you are reading this book, then it's probably safe to assume that you have not only a genuine love of animals, but also—like many other helping professionals—high levels of empathy and compassion. The ability to identify so strongly with the suffering of animals is often what leads us down this career path, but it also causes us to put the needs of others ahead of our own. Indeed, many of us who work with animals would describe it more as a calling than a career choice. For some, it's a passion; for many, a lifestyle. In her book *When Helping Hurts* (2013), grief recovery specialist Dr. Kathleen Ayl writes, "When you have compassion, you do not just 'feel' something, you also 'do' something. Compassion focuses those empathetic or sympathetic feelings and puts them into action."

After a full day of taking care of animals, you may return home and tend to your own furry, finned, and feathered friends. Maybe you've devoted your life to ending animal cruelty, and you write letters, sign petitions, participate in protests, or follow a strict vegan diet. Or perhaps you spend your free time picking up stray dogs or helping feral cats. Although this lifestyle is commendable, it sometimes lacks balance. In other words, people who love animals tend to be "on the clock," working up to twenty-four hours a day, seven days a week. Unsurprisingly, this kind of schedule can not only drain you but also make you vulnerable to compassion fatigue.

Are you curious about your own personality? Check out the website http://www.humanmetrics.com/personality/type to take your free personality test! In case you're wondering, I'm an INFJ, which stands for *I*ntrovert, i*N*tuitive, *F*eeling, and *J*udging.

Empathy and the Highly Sensitive Personality

I have a confession about my own personality, and it may resonate with some of you. Let me set the stage with a story. One day, back in college, my friend and I were walking around campus on our break, and it had just finished raining. It had rained so hard, in fact, that a bunch of snails had wandered onto the sidewalks in search of dry land. Some of the snails were headed toward the street, but some had already been crushed by passersby. To save the remaining lot, I carefully picked up every snail I could find and placed them on patches of dry grass. Ever since I can remember, I can't help but feel empathy for all creatures, great and small. I have such an acute awareness of the suffering of others that I seem to soak it up like a sponge. All my life, I have been told that I'm too sensitive, too shy, too emotional, too quiet, too this, and too that. I used to take those comments to heart, and I let them define me—as a weak and flawed person.

All that changed when I read Dr. Elaine Aron's amazing book, *The Highly Sensitive Person* (1996). Instead of pathologizing my sensitive traits, such as my extreme empathy, the book shed new light on what is simply a type of personality. Don't get me wrong— having a highly sensitive personality is not without its challenges, but Aron shows us that we can accept and embrace our sensitivity to make it work to our advantage rather than against us. Above all, she assures us that we are indeed "normal" and that, more importantly, we are not alone. If you feel like you may have a highly sensitive personality, then I encourage you to take this self-test at http://www.hsperson.com/test/.

Exposure to Trauma

A veterinary receptionist consoles a grief-stricken client. An animal-control officer spends the night alongside firefighters bringing out the charred remains of family pets after a fatal house fire. An investigator uncovers unspeakable abuse at a puppy mill. Unfortunately, these types of traumatic experiences are all too common in the field of animal welfare, and while they give you the fuel to fight for animals, it's important that you don't let these tragedies extinguish your flame.

Many of us have experienced trauma in one form or another at some point in our lives. Sexual assault, a car accident, childhood abuse, the death of a loved one, and even having to euthanize animals are all examples of primary trauma, which amounts to direct, personal exposure to a traumatic event. Indirect or secondary trauma refers to exposure to the suffering of others. This occurs often in animal welfare because you constantly witness or hear about traumatic events. While you may understand the traumatic stress brought on by the duties of a euthanasia technician, it's important that we don't discount the feelings of the adoption counselor or kennel attendant who cares for and falls in love with an animal one day only to find it gone the next, or the pet sitter or dog walker that grieves the loss of a long-time client's pet.

How exactly does trauma relate to compassion fatigue? According to Figley, in his book *Compassion Fatigue: Coping with Secondary Traumatic Stress Disorder in Those Who Treat the Traumatized* (1995), compassion fatigue is "identical to secondary stress disorder and the equivalent to PTSD." In other words, you may display some of the symptoms associated with PTSD, such as intrusive memories; nightmares; flashbacks; avoidance of thoughts, feelings, or external reminders related to the trauma; persistent negative thoughts or emotions; and hypervigilance. It has been suggested that having a personal history of trauma can increase your chances of developing compassion fatigue (Killian 2008). If this is the case for you, then I strongly recommend that you find a qualified therapist to help you work through any unresolved traumas from your past. See chapter nine for more detailed information on professional help.

Trauma and the Brain

The brain has the amazing ability to change itself. From our conception to the time we reach old age, our brains are continuously reorganizing their functions, connections, and neural pathways. This process, known as neuroplasticity, is what allows us to grow, learn, and adapt to our environments (Klorer 2005; Siegel 2010). In the right circumstances, our brains can flourish; negative events, however, including abuse, neglect, and other forms of trauma, can also alter the structure of the brain and take a toll on neuroplasticity. Not only does this negative plasticity cause parts of the brain to shrink, but it also leaves trauma survivors to struggle with chronic anxiety, depression, and a host of other emotional and cognitive impairments. The good news is that positive experiences have the power to alter the brain too:

- Psychotherapy can be a very powerful tool in the facilitation of positive plasticity and is helpful for a variety of symptoms and disorders, such as depression, panic disorder, and obsessive-compulsive disorder. Learn more about psychotherapy in chapter nine.
- Research suggests that engaging in such creative expression as dance, drama, art, and music has helped to promote neuroplasticity (Kraybill 2015). Ways for you to get your creative juices flowing are outlined in chapter seven.
- Another effective activity is simply taking a walk. In fact, taking a brisk walk in an interesting place actually exercises the brain and increases gray matter (Doidge 2015). We'll discuss the additional benefits of walking in chapter five.
- Just as physical exercise can help to build muscle, mental exercises can boost brain growth. For example, the present-centered form of meditation known as mindfulness can help with positive plasticity (Wolkin 2015). We'll explore mindfulness in chapter four.

- Research suggests that the practice of yoga may help with brain growth (Froeliger et al. 2012). In fact, yoga, along with mindfulness and other forms of meditation, has been increasingly studied and implemented as a treatment for veterans struggling with PTSD (Libby et al. 2012). Check out chapter five for more information on yoga.
- While I don't recommend it as a first line of defense or a replacement for therapy, some evidence does propose that antidepressant medications may have a positive impact on plasticity (Andrade 2010).

From music to meditation to medication, these practices provide hope for trauma survivors. By having an understanding of how plasticity affects our brains, both negatively and positively, we can gain better insight into the devastation caused by trauma—and the miracle of the brain's ability to bring us back from it.

Professional Burnout

Burnout refers to the emotional, physical, and mental exhaustion that can result from experiencing chronic stress on the job. Over time, it can eat away at your confidence and undermine your sense of accomplishment, leaving you feeling cynical, ineffective, and overall dissatisfied with the work you do. If left unchecked, burnout can end up overwhelming people to the point that they have to leave their jobs and sometimes even the entire profession. But there is a significant difference between burnout and compassion fatigue. Basically, anyone can burn out during his or her career: plumbers can burn out, stockbrokers can burn out, and waitresses can burn out. But when you take a highly stressful work environment and add the empathy factor commonly found in animal welfare and other helping professions, this can result in burnout and/or compassion fatigue. In fact, both burnout and compassion fatigue share many of the same symptoms:

- feeling fatigued or exhausted
- having trouble sleeping
- feeling cynical, angry, or irritable

- being less productive at work
- lacking joy in and satisfaction for your work
- feeling sad, apathetic, or hopeless
- developing physical ailments
- employing unhelpful coping skills

A number of factors can contribute to career burnout, including the following:

- **A Toxic Work Environment:** The work you do is hard enough, but when you add a hint of drama and a dash of dysfunction into the mix—such as negative coworkers, a micromanaging boss, a workplace bully, office politics, or simply too much gossip—it can wind up being the perfect recipe for burnout.
- **Lack of Control:** This can include everything from crazy work schedules and ambiguous job expectations to a lack of support from superiors and not having the proper tools for the job.
- **Poor Support System:** You and your animal-welfare colleagues have a demanding job that entails certain stressors the general public can't readily relate to. Therefore, having adequate social support is crucial when it comes to keeping compassion fatigue and burnout at bay. In fact, a study by Etzion (1984) looked at the connection between burnout and social support and found that the latter can significantly reduce the effects of workplace stress.
- **Not Enough Balance:** We're going to talk about bringing balance into your life a lot throughout this workbook. Trying to juggle work demands—long hours, inflexible schedules, and being on call—and your personal life can be challenging, but believe me, nothing will send you spiraling into stress-induced burnout faster than not making time for yourself.

How Compassion Fatigue Develops

So how do we go from energized to exhausted? Compassion fatigue doesn't happen overnight. In fact, Baranowsky and Gentry (2010) suggest that compassion fatigue actually falls on a trajectory or follows five progressive phases, which I have adapted here to reflect the nature of the animal-welfare field:

Zealot Phase

- We feel enthusiastic and excited.
- We are committed to the cause.
- We are involved and go all out to make a difference.

Irritability Phase

- We may start to cut corners.
- We may begin to make mistakes.
- We may distance ourselves from family, friends, and coworkers.

Withdraw Phase

- Our once-enthusiastic attitude turns to anger and bitterness.
- We start to neglect loves ones and ourselves.
- The protective walls start to go up.

Zombie Phase

- We may feel disconnected from our own feelings or thoughts.
- We begin to run on autopilot.
- We may even feel like we've lost our compassion.

Pathology-and-Victimization Phase versus Maturation-and-Renewal Phase

- We either become so overwhelmed that we leave the field, or we develop resiliency skills to continue the fight.

Where Do You Stand?

It's important that we don't view compassion fatigue in terms of black and white—it's not like you either have it or you don't. It's better to think of compassion fatigue as landing on a continuum or in the gray area. In other words, it's a matter of scope. If I have compassion fatigue, to what extent do I have it? Do I have a mild case that I can nip in the bud or am I teetering on a complete meltdown? I should also mention that many of the symptoms of compassion fatigue are similar to those of clinical depression, anxiety disorders, and even PTSD, and a mental-health therapist can help you determine if you're struggling with a more severe condition. We'll explore getting professional help more in chapter nine.

To help you further understand compassion fatigue and how it may affect you, I invite you to visit http://proqol.org/ProQol_Test.html. There, you will find a self-test developed by trauma experts Charles Figley and Beth Stamm (2009–2012). The ProQol (Professional Quality of Life) test measures compassion satisfaction, or the enjoyment that you get from your work, as well as compassion fatigue, which Stamm breaks down into two components: burnout and secondary trauma. I encourage you to take the test before you continue reading, after you've completed the workbook, and again in six months. Incidentally, when taking the test, you may want to replace the words "person" and "people" with "animal" or "animals" where appropriate.

CHAPTER 3
The Human-Animal Bond

*Nothing compares to a cat's purr when you are
stressed or upset, and nothing can calm you down
better than a cat on your lap looking for attention.*
—ANN WORTINGER, LICENSED VETERINARY
TECHNICIAN, MICHIGAN

Animals in Antiquity

Since the dawn of time, humans have shared their lives with animals. Historical evidence from around the globe suggests that many ancient civilizations valued animals for far more than just their herding, hunting, or protective abilities. In Egypt, for example, cats were cherished and kept as pets, and dogs were mummified upon death and honored as guides in the afterlife (Ikram 2005). The remains of a human skeleton buried alongside a young wolf puppy in Israel date back twelve thousand years (National Institutes of Health 2009). In more recent history, we have seen increasing efforts to provide animals with legal protection, the most notable case in the United States being the birth of the American Society of for the Prevention of Cruelty to Animals (ASPCA) in 1866. And while I believe that we still have a long way to go, laws currently exist in all fifty states, as well as at the national level, to protect domestic animals, wildlife, and (to some extent) livestock.

All in the Family

Today, around 65 percent of us in the United States share our home with at least one companion animal, anything from hamsters to horses and everything in between. As a nation we spent more than sixty billion dollars on our critters in 2015, which is more than double the amount at the turn of the century (American Pet Products Association 2016). Animals provide us with nonjudgmental and unconditional love, so it's no wonder that so many pet parents consider their furry, finned, or feathered friends family members! When we live with, care for, work with, or have a role in protecting animals, we often find ourselves forming deep attachments to them. This special connection, known as the human-animal bond, is described by the American Veterinary Medical Association (2016) as a "mutual beneficial and dynamic relationship between people and animals that is influenced by behaviors that are essential to the health and well-being of both."

Benefits of the Human-Animal Bond

People are forming friendships with creatures great and small in some rather unlikely places, including hospitals and even prisons. The company of birds helps older patients in skilled rehab facilities battle loneliness and depression while boosting morale (Jessen et al. 1996). Aquariums full of fish promote healthy eating habits, sociability, and relaxation among dementia patients (Filan et al. 2006). Prison programs are becoming increasingly popular, offering second chances to inmates and animals alike (Rhoades 2001). From dogs and horses that need socialization to injured, sick, and orphaned wildlife, animals of all kinds are receiving comfort and care in the confinements of penitentiary walls and returning the favor by providing inmates with a purpose.

Research has only begun to uncover the myriad of psychological, physiological, and social benefits from human-animal interactions. Did you know that petting a dog, for instance, has been shown to reduce blood pressure (Vormbrock et al. 1988). In addition to helping us calm down, our critters can help decrease our heart rate and cholesterol levels, reduce depression, and boost our immune system (Time 2014). And forget those fad diets and magic weight-loss pills. When it comes to the battle of the bulge, nothing beats man's best friend. A study by the National Institutes of Health (2009) revealed that those of us who walk our dogs on a regular basis are more active, less obese, and even more social. Animals promote healing in hospitalized children, aid adults coping with chronic health conditions like cancer, and bring peace to those in hospice care by alleviating their anxiety and decreasing their discomfort (Geisler 2004). As you can see from the following cases, animals have an amazing ability to heal us:

- Pets can help children develop motor skills, self-confidence, and empathy.
- Children often see their pets as companions or even siblings. In withdrawn or shy children, sometimes a pet is their *only* companion.
- Pets provide us with affection.
- They afford us opportunities to exercise, play, and socialize.
- Companion animals allow us to love and nurture something, which can lead to enhanced self-esteem.
- They depend on us, which creates caregiving opportunities.
- Pets can offer stability and support in difficult situations, such as during a divorce or move.
- They can serve as an extension (eyes, ears, or legs) for those with physical impairments.
- Pets can be a lifeline for people with terminal illnesses.
- For the elderly especially, pets can provide a sense of purpose.
- Service and emotional support dogs are increasingly being used as a complementary treatment for PTSD in returning soldiers.

When the Bond is Severed

Because animals hold such a special place in our hearts, it's easy to see how we can bond with them, both on a personal and professional level. But what does this all have to do with compassion fatigue? When you work in the animal-welfare field, you are bound to form deep attachments to some of the critters in your care, which can also make you vulnerable to the grief that can result when that bond is broken. "Everyone has patients and clients that they become very attached to, and an unfortunate part of our job is that pets do not live forever," says Ann Wortinger, a vet tech from Michigan. "Having to say goodbye to a cherished friend is hard." Given companion animals' short life-spans, veterinarians lose their patients at a much higher rate—five times that of their human doctor counterparts (Tremayne 2010).

From the top down, all levels of an organization can feel the impact of grief. Not only do veterinarians and their staffs have to deal with the heartache of losing their patients, but they also have the task of trying to comfort grieving clients. Keep in mind that grief in the workplace isn't unique to animal hospitals. To demonstrate this point, take a moment to imagine this scenario: An animal-control officer confiscates a large number of animals from a hoarding situation. He brings them into the Humane Society where they are evaluated by a team of veterinarians, behaviorists, and other staff members. The team decides that the animals are either too sick or aggressive to be put up for adoption. One after another, the animals are put down by the shelter's euthanasia technician and her assistant. A young volunteer who is cleaning cages just outside the euthanasia room can't help but notice the assembly line of cats and dogs going to the cooler.

Casualties of War

Vulnerability to grief is especially a concern for those of you who perform or are exposed to euthanasia. Just like everyone else in the animal welfare field, veterinarians and euthanasia techs often devote their lives to helping sick, injured, homeless, abused, and neglected animals—but often pay a high price for doing so. Those who are charged with the task are more prone to depression, inappropriate emotions, physical illness, substance abuse, unresolved grief, and even suicide. As I mentioned earlier, around 17 percent of veterinarians in this nation have thought about suicide. This concern isn't limited to the United States; similar results have been found all over the globe (Larkin 2015). Given the constant difficulty of having to end the lives of the very creatures they strive to protect combined with the social stigma surrounding euthanasia (particularly in shelters), professionals like vets, animal-control officers, and euthanasia techs are faced with "moral stressors" on an almost daily basis (Reeve et al. 2005).

I am sad to report that, just before this book went to print, the animal-welfare community lost one of its soldiers—Dr. Jian Zhicheng. According to reports, the veterinarian and director of a Taiwanese animal shelter took her own life in early May of 2016 after being cyberbullied because of her role as a euthanasia technician. Zhicheng, a vocal advocate for adoption, had reportedly already been depressed and guilt-ridden over having to put animals down. She gave herself a lethal injection of the very same drug used to euthanize animals and died five days later (Williams 2016).

Confessions of a Killer

It had been a typical day at the shelter when I was called over the loud-speaker to the ER, a public-friendly code word for the euthanasia room. I was met by my assistant and a frail, elderly man holding his equally frail and elderly dog. We shuffled into the small, cinderblock-walled room, and he put his beloved companion on the table. I placed the needle into the dog's tiny vein, as I had done many times before, and within seconds, he was gone. When I offered the man some time alone with his dog, he burst into tears. He told me that he had recently lost his wife of fifty years and that the dog was all he had left to live for. As emotional as this moment was, I was able to keep it together and offered the grief-stricken man all I could: a sympathetic ear. But when he pulled out a small toy from his coat pocket and nuzzled it under the dog's lifeless head, it took all the strength I had to keep my composure. The man hugged me on his way out and thanked me for my kindness. I could feel the tears welling up in my eyes.

As soon as he was out of sight, I lost it. I huddled in the corner of the room and wept like a baby. At that moment, all of the walls I had built up in order to do this job day after day suddenly gave way and came crashing down around me. I cried that day not only for the man who had lost his dog but also for all the lives I had taken for no good reason: litters upon litters of pit bull pups that were destroyed to keep them out of the city's fighting rings, the cats whose only crime was their "old" age, the "after-Easter rush" of unwanted bunnies whose novelty had worn off, the animals who had been abused or neglected to the point of no return, whose eyes begged us to put them out of their suffering.

Friends and relatives outside the shelter often asked me how I could do such a painful job. Let me set the record straight, and speak on behalf of everyone that performs euthanasia: we love animals to the point of exhaustion. We sign up for this incredibly painful job because we care. We stare into the eyes of the unloved, the unwanted, and the throwaways. We feel their pain. And so, yes, sometimes we have to end their lives. But we allow them to die with dignity. We allow them to take their last breath in the loving arms of overworked, overwhelmed, underpaid, and undervalued workers who are teetering on the edge of a breakdown—and who love them more than you can possibly comprehend. Looking back, that is exactly what I did, and I have no regrets. We do the best we can, and sometimes the best way to save an animal is to let them go.

How to Cope with Personal or Workplace Grief

So how can you avoid burnout and still remain compassionate? While society is a long way from solving the pet-overpopulation epidemic, those of you who dedicate your lives to being part of the solution will be more effective if you can learn how to deal with the occupational hazards inherent in the animal-welfare field, including euthanasia. By managing stress, developing appropriate coping skills, practicing self-care, and seeking out support, you can minimize your chances of falling victim to compassion fatigue while increasing your awareness, understanding, and self-esteem (Ross and Baron-Sorensen 2007). It's also critical that you be allowed to express your feelings openly and honestly, receive validation, and educate yourself on the stages of grief. If not dealt with, grief can eat away at you, and the stress that sometimes accompanies grief can hinder your relationships with other staff members, customers, clients, spouses, friends, and family members. By having a better understanding of the grief process, you'll be better equipped to ward off compassion fatigue and burnout.

The Stages of Grief

There are a variety of theoretical models of grief, but I have chosen the classic Kubler-Ross (1969) framework to give you an idea of what the grief process can look like. It's important to note that the grief process is not linear; it's more like a roller coaster. Some people do not always experience all of the following stages, nor do they necessarily experience them in this particular order:

- **Denial**
  Often the first stage of grief, denial may occur when we learn that an animal in our care is terminally ill, when a wave of parvo or UTI hits, and, of course, upon euthanasia. Usually short term, denial is a normal coping mechanism that protects you from shock as well as the sadness that soon follows.

- **Bargaining**
  Bargaining with God or another higher power, and even the animal itself, is common in grief.
- **Anger**
  You may find yourself angry with coworkers, clients, veterinarians, the general public, God, or another higher power.
- **Sorrow**
  Eventually, sadness takes over, and it can affect many aspects of your life. This is a time for tears, and you may experience trouble sleeping or eating. As tough as it is, however, sorrow is actually the healing stage.
- **Resolution**
  This final stage provides you with the realization and acceptance that the animal is gone. You will get through this.

Guilt

I'd also like to say a word about guilt. Although not technically a stage of grief, guilt is perhaps one of the strongest emotions felt across the board in animal welfare. I used to be saturated with guilt. I felt guilty every time I euthanized an animal. I felt guilty on the rare occasions I took a vacation. I felt guilty when I couldn't adopt any more animals. I felt guilty when I was at home because I wasn't at work helping animals, and I felt guilty when I was at work because I wasn't at home with my own animals. I felt guilty when I turned in my badge and ended my career in humane law enforcement so that I could go back to school. And I felt guilty because I couldn't save my beloved parrot's life. As you can clearly see, guilt can really hinder the grieving process and is perhaps the biggest roadblock to healing. When I feel like I'm struggling with guilt, I remember what my husband once said to me, and now I'm passing his wise words on to you: "You do more for animals in one day than most people do in a lifetime."

Complicated Grief

Remember, grieving for an animal is normal and may be as intense as grieving for a human—if not more. But what if we experience grief that goes beyond the norm? Although the bereavement process is very unique and personal, complicated grief, a severe and chronic type of grief, is fairly common with pet loss. Signs that you may be struggling with complicated grief include the following:

- the inability to accept the animal's death
- intrusive thoughts or flashbacks
- nightmares about the animal's death
- continuous yearning or searching for the animal
- persistent, uncontrollable crying after several weeks or months
- sleep disturbances, such as insomnia
- an increase or decrease in appetite
- social isolation
- hindered work or school performance
- substance abuse
- feeling suicidal or homicidal

If not dealt with, complicated grief can lead to an increased risk of developing symptoms associated with depression, anxiety, and even posttraumatic stress disorder. But there is help. Fortunately, society is becoming more aware of the very real and very painful effects of pet loss, and a variety of resources are now available for those grieving the loss of an animal, including books, online forums, support groups, and pet loss therapists.

People often ask me how to get over their grief. My response is that you don't get over, you get through. There's no way around it: the only way through grief is through grief. In order to do that, you must allow yourself to feel the myriad of emotions that accompany bereavement. To help you understand your own experiences with grief, answer the following questions openly and honestly:

I am struggling with denial right now over the loss of

_____

I feel

_____

I am struggling with anger right now over the loss of

_____

I feel

_____

I am struggling with bargaining right now over the loss of

_____

I feel

_____

I am struggling with sorrow right now over the loss of

_____

I feel

_____

I am struggling with guilt right now over the loss of

_____

I feel

_____

What was your first experience with death?

_____

_____

Were you allowed to grieve? Describe how your family, your culture, or larger society influenced how you handled grief.

_____

_____

How did that experience shape how you deal with death today?

_____

_____

Do you have any particular religious/spiritual beliefs about death?

_____

_____

Starfish Stories: a Porcine Paradise

He fought as a marine in Vietnam. He battled blazes as a firefighter. But the most challenging job Richard Hoyle has ever taken on, he says, comes in the form of caring for roughly 135 pigs. Hoyle, along with his wife, is the founder of the Pig Preserve, a sanctuary located in the middle of rural Tennessee. What began with one pot-bellied pig eventually turned into a safe haven for more than two hundred rescued miniature pigs—but that was just the beginning. Hoyle's life changed forever when he learned about the horrific abuse of pigs in the meat industry. "Babe was a crippled young farm pig who had been rescued off of the 'dead pile' at a factory farm because she had a nonfunctioning rear leg," Hoyle says.

Today, the sanctuary provides refuge for these one thousand-pound-plus gentle giants and their feral cousins. "We realized that these pigs were social, nomadic herd animals, and to be truly happy, they needed more than pens or tiny pastures to have any kind of quality of life," Hoyle says. "Our dream became to create a preserve where our rescued pigs could be free to live life on their terms, as Mother Nature intended them to live."

And while that dream came to fruition in early 2006, it hasn't been without its challenges. For Hoyle, there are no vacations, no sick days, no weekends off. "The pigs must be fed and cared for 365 days a year...it is an unrelenting responsibility that consumes your every waking moment," Hoyle says. But it's not the sultry summers or bitter-cold winters that take a toll on Hoyle. It's not his aging body or the grief that comes with the inevitable loss of his beloved pigs. What haunts him the most is a challenge that many animal rescuers face, which is the ability to keep the Pig Preserve going financially. Because the sanctuary is funded by donations and an occasional grant, the quest to find donors and supporters is a never-ending job for Hoyle. And the pressure weighs heavy on his heart. "Without the funds to feed and care for the pigs, the sanctuary would go bankrupt and the animals would pay the ultimate price for our failure," Hoyle says.

Despite the financial challenges, not to mention the physical and emotional struggles, this is Hoyle's calling. He says that the joy he derives from rescuing pigs—when one of these timid and frightened souls finally takes an apple from his hand or drops to the ground for a belly rub—is indescribable. "Many of the pigs we have taken in have been through a living hell before they arrive here...many of them have been badly abused and virtually none of them have ever known anything except a tiny pen or a dark stall to live in," Hoyle says. "To watch one of these pigs step off the trailer and see acres of green grass, feel the sun on their backs for the first time, and realize they are free is one of the best feelings in the world."

If you would like to help support or learn more about the Pig Preserve, please visit http://www.thepigpreserve.org.

Part Two

CHAPTER 4
Relaxation Tools

*Everyone needs to take a time out. Whether it's going for
a long walk and enjoying nature, meditation, having a
good support system, or getting a massage—whatever
helps you emotionally, physically, and spiritually.*
−BETH, FORMER ANIMAL-CONTROL OFFICER, COLORADO

By managing stress, developing appropriate coping skills, practicing self-care, and seeking out support, you can minimize your chances of falling victim to compassion fatigue. At the same time, you can increase your compassion satisfaction, which is essentially the joy you get from protecting, caring for, working with, and/or loving animals. Chapter four is the first of the tools chapters. At this point, I want you to imagine that you've just been given an imaginary toolbox. As you learn each technique, put it in your toolbox. It's not one single coping skill or exercise that will help you combat compassion fatigue but a combination of tools. By the time you have finished reading this workbook, it is my hope that you will have a full toolbox from which to pick and choose the strategies that work best for you when you need them the most.

Mindfulness
This method is helpful for

- anxiety
- depression

- sleep
- stress

Have you ever noticed that, as a culture, we tend to either ruminate about the past or worry about the future? Or that we walk around like zombies on autopilot? How often do we actually live in the moment? If your answer is not very often, then mindfulness is for you. Founded by Jon Kabat-Zinn (1994), mindfulness is the art of "paying attention in a particular way; on purpose, in the present moment; and nonjudgmentally." I first learned how to practice mindfulness in grad school, from a wise professor who described it as "eastern philosophy meets western science." Every night before class, he would guide us in a mindfulness activity to help us clear our heads so that we would be fully present and prepared for learning. And it worked.

Mindfulness, which has its roots in early meditation practices, has been backed by modern day scientists and is now enjoying increasing mainstream popularity. It's no wonder since mindfulness has been shown to reduce stress, anxiety, and depression, as well as help with chronic pain, sleep, and quieting the mind (Corliss 2015). When we learn to be mindful, we can then let go of many of the negative thoughts and emotions that often prevent us from living a truly happy and fulfilling life.

Meditation and Beyond

Unlike some types of meditation, whose goal is to completely rid the mind of any thoughts, mindfulness meditation encourages you to simply notice your thoughts, without judgment. But mindfulness need not be limited to meditation. Mindfulness can be practiced virtually anytime, anywhere. We can eat mindfully, drive mindfully, walk mindfully, and work mindfully. Wherever you are, try this simple mindfulness exercise:

1. *Observe* what you're doing. Are you standing, sitting, or lying down? Notice with all your senses. Notice how your feet feel against the ground, or how your body feels against the chair, for example. Notice the way the air smells. Notice how it feels as you breathe in and out. Notice the temperature of the air and how it feels against

your skin. Notice what you hear around you. Take in every little sound. Look around and notice—really notice—what you see.

2. *Describe* what you notice. Instead of using judging words like "good" or "bad" or "comfortable" or "uncomfortable," use descriptive words and phrases, such as "soft," "blue," or "warm" or "birds chirping" or "gentle breeze."

3. *Accept* your thoughts. If you're struggling with an intrusive thought, don't try to force it out of your head; just observe that you had a thought and then gently bring your mind back to the present moment.

Mindful Deep Breathing
This method helps with

- anger
- anxiety
- depression
- insomnia
- stress
- tension

When my clients come to me presenting with chronic anxiety, depression, or other emotional problems, one of the first skills I teach them is how to breathe correctly. This may sound strange, but there is actually a right and a wrong way to breathe! You see, when you're under a lot of stress, your body goes into a protective state called fight or flight. Basically, you release certain hormones that cause of variety of changes in your body, including increased heart rate, muscle tension, and rapid breathing. From an evolutionary perspective, these bodily changes certainly served our ancestors well in a time when danger lurked around every corner. Today, however, living in this constant state of arousal is not only unnecessary, but it can also have harmful effects on your health and well-being. The good news is that you can actually trick your brain out of fight or flight and into relaxation mode with abdominal breathing. According to the American Institute of Stress (2012), when practiced daily for twenty to thirty minutes, abdominal or belly breathing increases the amount of oxygen sent to the brain while reducing overall anxiety and stress.

Top Tip

- If you're having a hard time breathing through your belly, then lie down and place a small plastic or paper cup on your stomach. As you inhale, try to make the cup rise and fall with each breath. As an alternative, try to imagine that you have a balloon in your belly and, with each breath, you're inflating that balloon.

The Technique

1. To begin, sit or lie down in a comfortable position and close your eyes.
2. Take a slow, deep breath in through your nose. Notice the sensation of the air flowing in and out.
3. For deep relaxation, try to exhale a second or two longer than you inhale. For example, breathe in for three seconds, and then breathe out for five seconds.
4. As you begin to breathe more deeply, notice how the air fills your belly first and then your chest. As you slowly exhale, notice how the air leaves your chest and then your belly.
5. If you notice any distracting thoughts coming to mind, I want you to simply notice them. Don't judge them or force them out of your mind; just notice them and bring your mind back to your breathing.
6. You may start to notice your surroundings on a more heightened level—the temperature of the room, the ticking of a clock, the rumble of traffic outside, or the way your body feels against the chair or bed. Again, I want you to notice these sensations without judging them, and then bring your mind back to your breathing.
7. Now, I want you to slow your breathing down a bit further. Slowly count with each inhalation and exhalation—one, two, three, four—and feel your body relax even more with each breath.

8. When you feel comfortable, I want you to open your eyes and take notice of how your body feels.

To get the maximum benefit of mindful deep breathing, you'll want to practice for at least twenty minutes per day. But don't be afraid to start small—get in the habit of practicing for just five minutes a day, and then gradually increase your time. You may want to use the following worksheet to keep track of how mindful deep breathing helps you feel. For each day listed below, rate how you feel both before and after practicing mindful deep breathing by using the following rating scale:

1—None   2—Low   3—Moderate   4—High   5—Severe

Monday	**Before**	**After**
Anger	_____	_____
Anxiety	_____	_____
Depression	_____	_____
Insomnia	_____	_____
Stress	_____	_____
Tension	_____	_____

Tuesday	**Before**	**After**
Anger	_____	_____
Anxiety	_____	_____
Depression	_____	_____
Insomnia	_____	_____
Stress	_____	_____
Tension	_____	_____

Wednesday	**Before**	**After**
Anger	_____	_____
Anxiety	_____	_____
Depression	_____	_____

	Before	After
Insomnia	_____	_____
Stress	_____	_____
Tension	_____	_____

Thursday	**Before**	**After**
Anger	_____	_____
Anxiety	_____	_____
Depression	_____	_____
Insomnia	_____	_____
Stress	_____	_____
Tension	_____	_____

Friday	**Before**	**After**
Anger	_____	_____
Anxiety	_____	_____
Depression	_____	_____
Insomnia	_____	_____
Stress	_____	_____
Tension	_____	_____

Saturday	**Before**	**After**
Anger	_____	_____
Anxiety	_____	_____
Depression	_____	_____
Insomnia	_____	_____
Stress	_____	_____
Tension	_____	_____

Sunday	**Before**	**After**
Anger	_____	_____
Anxiety	_____	_____
Depression	_____	_____

Insomnia   _____   _____
Stress   _____   _____
Tension   _____   _____

Progressive Muscle Relaxation

This method is helpful for

- anger
- anxiety
- insomnia
- stress
- tension

As I've mentioned in earlier chapters, those of you in caregiving roles typically focus on helping others so much that you may tend to ignore your own needs. Even when your body is desperately trying to tell you something—in the form of headaches, back problems, and/or tight muscles—you may not always hear the message.

One of my favorite ways to reduce tension and relax is through a technique called progressive muscle relaxation. With practice, you can use this stress buster almost anywhere, anytime. Some people like to begin the day with this exercise while others (like me) enjoy it just before bedtime. Do whatever works best for you, but remember: it takes practice to become more in tune with your body and train your muscles to relax. Like you do with mindful deep breathing, try to practice progressive muscle relaxation on a daily basis. But please consult with your doctor if you have any medical issues or injuries that may cause pain.

Helpful Hints

- When first learning progressive muscle relaxation, set aside a special time and place to practice, free from any distractions, such as loud noise or bright light.
- Do not practice after drinking alcohol or eating a large meal.

- Remember to use mindful deep breathing throughout the exercise.
- Count to ten while tensing each muscle, release immediately, and then count to twenty before moving on.
- Each time you relax a muscle, you might say something, such as "relax" or "let it go."

The Technique

1. Sit or lie down in a comfortable, relaxed position. If possible, remove your shoes, and close your eyes.
2. Set the stage for relaxation by taking in a few deep belly breaths.
3. Make a fist with your right hand, as if you're squeezing the juice out of a lemon, and then relax.
4. Now, tense your right bicep by bringing your forearm up to up to your shoulder, just as you would if you were lifting a dumbbell, and then relax.
5. Repeat the above with your left hand and then your left arm, and then relax.
6. Now for some facial exercises. Raise your eyebrows up high, and then relax.
7. Shut your eyes and scrunch up your face, and then relax.
8. Open your mouth as wide as you can, and then relax.
9. Give your neck a gentle stretch by very carefully rolling it from side to side.
10. Shrug your shoulders as if you're trying to touch them to your ears, and then relax.
11. Stick out your chest and squeeze your shoulder blades together, and then relax.
12. Would you believe that we hold stress in our buttocks? Squeeze those glutes, and then relax.
13. Tense your upper right leg. Make your quad as hard as a rock, and then relax.
14. Very slowly, extend your right leg, lift your right foot, and point your toes toward you. Now relax.

15. Repeat with your left leg, and then relax.
16. Curl your toes under on your right foot, and then relax.
17. Do the same with your left foot. Now relax.
18. Finally, take a moment to mentally scan your body from head to toe and notice any remaining tension. If needed, tense and relax those muscles again. Take a few more deep, cleansing breaths, and, when you're ready, open your eyes.

You may want to use the following worksheet to keep track of how progressive muscle relaxation makes you feel. For each day below, rate how you feel both before and after practicing progressive muscle relaxation by using the following rating scale:

1—None   2—Low   3—Moderate   4—High   5—Severe

Monday	**Before**	**After**
Anger	_____	_____
Anxiety	_____	_____
Insomnia	_____	_____
Stress	_____	_____
Tension	_____	_____

Tuesday	**Before**	**After**
Anger	_____	_____
Anxiety	_____	_____
Insomnia	_____	_____
Stress	_____	_____
Tension	_____	_____

Wednesday	**Before**	**After**
Anger	_____	_____
Anxiety	_____	_____

Insomnia   _____   _____
Stress   _____   _____
Tension   _____   _____

Thursday	**Before**	**After**

Anger   _____   _____
Anxiety   _____   _____
Insomnia   _____   _____
Stress   _____   _____
Tension   _____   _____

Friday	**Before**	**After**

Anger   _____   _____
Anxiety   _____   _____
Insomnia   _____   _____
Stress   _____   _____
Tension   _____   _____

Saturday	**Before**	**After**

Anger   _____   _____
Anxiety   _____   _____
Insomnia   _____   _____
Stress   _____   _____
Tension   _____   _____

Sunday	**Before**	**After**

Anger   _____   _____
Anxiety   _____   _____
Insomnia   _____   _____
Stress   _____   _____
Tension   _____   _____

Guided Meditation

This method helps with

- anxiety
- depression
- insomnia
- irritability
- stress
- tension

If you are like many people who can't seem to turn off the chatter in your head, then you may find that guided mediation is an easy and effective way to slow down and clear your mind. With the use of guided imagery and soothing music, guided mediation allows you achieve deep relaxation with very little effort, making it perfect for beginners and seasoned meditators alike. You can record the following script or have a friend or loved one read it to you, but I highly recommend that you download the audio recording, complete with soothing music, for free at deepwatermichigan.com. Do not listen to the recording while driving or performing any task which requires you to be alert.

The Island

Begin by taking in a slow, deep breath. Take a minute or two to slow your breathing and soften your muscles.

I want you to imagine that you are standing on a long, wooden dock, looking out over the water at the horizon. As morning breaks, you can see the sun gently start to peek over the hills and begin to illuminate the shimmering lake. As the sun continues to rise, you begin to see more clearly. You notice a pair of majestic white swans off in the distance. You can smell the aroma of the pine trees that line the shore. You hear birds singing from above you as they welcome the day. You take in a slow, deep breath of fresh morning air.

You notice a small white sailboat next to the dock. You decide to get in. As you untie the ropes and release yourself from the dock, the boat slowly begins to drift off over the beautiful blue water. As the waves carry you further and further out, you turn around to see the dock in the distance, but you feel completely safe and secure in your sailboat.

As the sun climbs higher and higher in the sky, you feel the warmth on your skin and feel comforted by its embrace. Every now and then, a gentle breeze cools your skin and fills the sail of your boat, allowing you to coast smoothly along the water. You reach over the side of the boat and dip your hand into the cool, crisp water. In this moment, you begin to notice your worries drifting away, as if they are being carried off by the gentle, rolling waves. In this moment, you are completely free. In this moment, you are free from any sadness, free from any doubts, free from any fears. In this moment, you are free to be yourself. You are free to drift anywhere you like in your sailboat.

As you drift along, you let go off all your worries. You let go of any distressing thoughts. You let go of any bad memories. You are slowly drifting toward a beautiful golden beach on a small, private island. When your boat reaches the shore, you get out to feel the soft, warm sand on your bare feet. You can hear native birds calling out to you to explore their island.

You take a breath of clean, fresh air and begin walking toward a clearing in the woods. You take the winding dirt path far into the forest. You are surrounded by strong, beautiful old trees, their branches gently dancing in the wind. You can smell the sweet fragrance of the wildflowers that line the path. As you continue down the path, you meet up with a gentle flowing stream. You bend down and cup your hands together in the crystal-clear water and take a drink. The water is so cool, so clean, and so refreshing. As you look up, you notice a deer standing at the water's edge with her baby. They look at you with big, beautiful brown eyes, but they are not afraid. They are as relaxed and calm as you are.

You are so relaxed and calm in this place that you decide to lie down in a patch of tall grass and wildflowers. You feel completely at peace and drift off for an afternoon nap. There is complete silence, and you feel safe and relaxed.

It is now time to awaken from your afternoon nap. As you slowly bring yourself to your feet, you can once again hear the sounds of the island—the gentle flowing stream and the birds flying overhead. You begin to follow the path back to the beach, where your sailboat awaits you. As you make your way through the woods, you feel happy and relaxed.

You finally reach the beach and climb into your sailboat. A strong yet gentle breeze fills your sail, and you begin your journey back across the lake. You don't even have to steer the boat—it seems to know exactly where to go. Your journey is peaceful and effortless.

Your trusty sailboat has now reached the dock. You step out and tie up your boat, knowing that it will always be there for you whenever you need it. You are home now. Gently bring your awareness back to your surroundings. When you feel comfortable, open your eyes.

You may want to use the following worksheet to keep track of how guided meditation makes you feel. For each day below, rate how you feel both before and after practicing guided meditation by using the following rating scale:

1—None   2—Low   3—Moderate   4—High   5—Intense

Monday	**Before**	**After**
Anxiety	_____	_____
Depression	_____	_____
Insomnia	_____	_____
Irritability	_____	_____
Stress	_____	_____
Tension	_____	_____

Tuesday	**Before**	**After**
Anxiety	_____	_____
Depression	_____	_____
Insomnia	_____	_____
Irritability	_____	_____
Stress	_____	_____
Tension	_____	_____

Wednesday	**Before**	**After**
Anxiety	_____	_____
Depression	_____	_____

Insomnia	_____	_____
Irritability	_____	_____
Stress	_____	_____
Tension	_____	_____

Thursday	**Before**	**After**
Anxiety	_____	_____
Depression	_____	_____
Insomnia	_____	_____
Irritability	_____	_____
Stress	_____	_____
Tension	_____	_____

Friday	**Before**	**After**
Anxiety	_____	_____
Depression	_____	_____
Insomnia	_____	_____
Irritability	_____	_____
Stress	_____	_____
Tension	_____	_____

Saturday	**Before**	**After**
Anxiety	_____	_____
Depression	_____	_____
Insomnia	_____	_____
Irritability	_____	_____
Stress	_____	_____
Tension	_____	_____

Sunday	**Before**	**After**
Anxiety	_____	_____
Depression	_____	_____

Insomnia	_____	_____
Irritability	_____	_____
Stress	_____	_____
Tension	_____	_____

Massage Therapy

This method is helpful for

- anxiety
- depression
- insomnia
- irritability
- stress
- tension
- trauma

The healing power of touch can be very beneficial and bring much relief if you're suffering from symptoms of compassion fatigue, according to Michigan-based massage therapist Christy Belolli. Therapeutic massage, she says, creates better blood flow throughout the body, leading to mental clarity and deep relaxation. "When you hold onto anxiety and stress, your muscles suffer; they become tight and hold onto toxins," Belolli says. "With massage, these toxins can be released from the muscles, especially with deeper body work."

Belolli stresses that taking care of yourself really needs to come first if you want to continue to take care of others. And although she recommends weekly massages in order to tend to your body's needs, she says that having body work done even just twice a month can be beneficial. "Making massage a necessity and scheduling that time for yourself can do wonders, both mentally and physically," Belolli says.

Cheyenne Walker couldn't agree more. As a Texas-based animal-control officer, she often feels physically and emotionally strained. "The very nature of the work is very demanding, both on my body and mind," says Walker, who decided to make weekly massages a part of her self-care plan about a year ago, around the same time that she quit smoking. "I realized I wanted to spend my money on improving my health, not destroying it. Getting a massage allows me to have something to look forward to all week. Plus it forces me to take care of myself."

Money-Saving Tips

- Keep an eye out for specials at massage clinics and spas.
- Check out your local college or massage school. Students gain hours by providing discounted—or even free—massages to the community.

Anger and Compassion Fatigue: How to Tame Your Dragon

Several years ago, while I was working at the local animal shelter, a good friend and coworker of mine came bursting through the door in a ball of furry, screaming, "I can't take this anymore!" I grabbed him by the arm and suggested we go outside to get some air. "If one more person surrenders an animal today, I'm going to jump across the counter and strangle them. I can't do this anymore. I just can't do this anymore!" he told me, as obscenities spewed from his mouth and tears streamed down his cheeks. I'm sure that you can understand his pain and frustration all too well.

Regardless of your role in animal welfare, chances are that you have to work with people. Dealing with the often-ignorant public can make your blood boil to the point of exhaustion and emotional breakdown. Anger, as you learned in chapter two, is a common symptom of compassion fatigue. But anger is also a normal emotion, often associated with other feelings, such as fear, sadness, guilt, shame, loneliness, or hurt. In fact, anger often inspires and motivates us to fight for positive change—such as animal rights. When emotions get the best of us, however, we can end up causing harm to both ourselves and others. So what should you do when you're pissed off at the world? To get a grip on your anger, it's helpful to first be able to identify some of your early warning signs, which may include the following:

- an increase in heart rate
- rapid or shallow breathing

- clenched fists or jaw
- tight muscles
- dizziness
- headache
- stomach ache
- trembling in the body or hands
- sweating
- sadness or anxiety
- pacing
- a hot face
- aggression
- throwing or hitting things
- crying
- becoming emotionally or physically abusive toward others
- yelling or screaming
- becoming very quiet
- using sarcasm
- frowning
- losing your sense of humor

Chances are that you first learned how to deal with anger as a child. Were you allowed to express your anger or were you forced to stuff it down? Did you witness or experience verbal or physical abuse and now find yourself exploding? It has been suggested that two common ways of dealing with anger—keeping it inside or expressing it by blowing up—can both actually harm you in the long run and have even been linked to an increase in heart disease (Bushman 2013). What's the best way to deal with anger? Let it go. The next time you need to tame your temper, try some of these techniques to help you release your rage:

- Count to ten or more.
- Listen to soothing music.
- Take a break or time-out.
- Use humor or laughter.
- Go for a walk, preferably outside.
- Draw or paint your anger.

- Relax with deep breathing.
- Practice assertive communication.
- Limit your exposure to violence, including in the media and video games.
- Write a letter, jotting down angry thoughts on a piece of paper, and then destroy it—tear it up, shred it, burn it, or bury it!
- Talk it out with a professional therapist.
- Join a support group.

To help you understand your anger even further, answer the following questions:

How did those in your family of origin express their anger?
_____
_____
_____

How do you currently express your anger?
_____
_____
_____

What are some of the things that trigger your anger?
_____
_____
_____

What are your anger warning signs?
_____
_____
_____

Have you ever experienced any negative consequences as a result of your anger?
_____
_____
_____

Which techniques are you willing to try so that you can handle your anger in a healthier way?

_____

_____

_____

CHAPTER 5
Let's Get Physical

I play hockey at my local hockey club, and I play saxophone in a jazz band. I find that physical exercise and playing music really help to manage deranged, unwelcome thoughts.
—KAROLYN, WILDLIFE REHABILITATOR AND FORENSICS HUMANE OFFICER, CALIFORNIA

Whenever I give workshops to animal-welfare groups, I always pick on someone in the audience and ask that person to name her dream car. That audience member always agrees with me that if she owned her dream car, whether a Mustang or a Mercedes, she would wash it often, fill it with premium gas, and give it regular tune-ups. Basically, she would baby it!

Well, why don't we treat ourselves in the same manner? This next chapter focuses on the physical ways in which we can take care of ourselves. By getting your body moving more, you'll discover how various activities can help to relieve many of the symptoms associated with compassion fatigue, including anger, anxiety, depression, insomnia, and stress.

Yoga
This activity helps alleviate

- anxiety
- depression

- stress
- trauma

When Jessica Johnson of New Mexico rolls out her yoga mat, she's preparing for more than just a good workout. Johnson, whose work involves creating systemic change through animal-protection laws, practices yoga in order to bring balance into her life when she's caught in the grips of compassion fatigue. "I'll occasionally struggle with feeling depressed or exhibiting a 'screw it all; it doesn't matter' attitude," Johnson says. "Yoga has helped me stave off the negativity and recharge. Challenging myself with difficult physical activity—and surviving it—usually makes me feel like I can handle anything, and then I'm ready to put my nose to the grindstone again."

Although you may tend to think of yoga as a relatively new, alternative practice, it actually has a long history of healing both the body and mind. In fact, the word yoga means "unite" and refers to the mind-body connection achieved through various poses, breath work, and meditation (Oren 2013). Incorporating yoga into our fast-paced lives forces us to slow down, relax, and simply be in the here and now. More importantly, yoga can help to make us feel more empowered. "I think that what's at the root of the emotional toll taken by so many animal welfare professionals and advocates is that we adopt the powerlessness that animals experience," says Johnson. "We should use things like yoga to remind ourselves that we *do* have power, our determination and steadfast work *will* produce results, and that we can't help animals if we are not healthy and vibrant ourselves." The health benefits—both physical and mental—of this ancient discipline are vast and include reduced stress, anxiety, chronic pain, and insomnia. Yoga also helps to boost metabolism; build muscle tone; and improve posture, strength, balance, and flexibility (Mayo Clinic 2016). With all that yoga has to offer, it's no wonder that it's been around since ancient times!

Money-Saving Tips

- Many yoga studios offer discounted trial classes for new clients.
- Check out the popular website meetup.com for free or inexpensive yoga meet-up groups in your area.

- Look for yoga classes held at your local YMCA, health club or gym, community center, church, or college.
- Once you've learned the correct form and some basic techniques from a qualified instructor, grab a good yoga book or DVD plus a mat and practice at home, in the park, or even at work on your lunch break.

Walking

This activity is beneficial for

- anger
- anxiety
- depression
- fatigue
- insomnia
- stress
- tension

One of the easiest, most affordable, and most effective ways to combat compassion fatigue and many of its associated symptoms is moving forward—literally. You know that walking and other forms of exercise are good for your body, but studies suggest that walking for just thirty minutes a day is also good for your mind (Sharma et al. 2006). How does getting physical help with mental health? Exercise, such as walking, allows the brain to release certain neurotransmitters or "feel good" chemicals. It also increases body temperature, which is thought to have a calming effect on the brain. According to the Anxiety and Depression Association of America (ADAA), daily walking and other forms of moderate exercise can help to alleviate depression and anxiety as well as decrease blood pressure, making it the perfect stress buster (2014). By helping to release a lot of the negative emotions associated with compassion fatigue, walking promotes mental clarity and positive thinking. It can boost self-esteem, increase energy levels, improve sleep quality (ADAA 2014), provide opportunities to socialize, and allow you to reconnect with the natural world.

Now, don't get me wrong: working out at the gym or hitting the treadmill is great, but I really encourage you to get moving outside as much as possible. Even if it's just fifteen minutes a day, your body will reap the benefits of natural sunlight. This is especially important in the winter months if you tend to get seasonal blues. To get the most from your walks, aim for thirty minutes on most days. Brisk walks in the morning are great if you struggle with insomnia, but even breaking down your walks into three ten-minute chunks can be effective. Personally, I have found that walking on my lunch break or taking a midafternoon stroll really helps me to maintain my energy levels throughout the day, not to mention that it lifts my mood. Do whatever works for you, and don't be afraid to start small. Make a commitment to walk for ten minutes a day, and then work your way up to a half hour. Setting and achieving healthy, realistic goals can really help to increase your motivation and self-esteem as well as set the stage for a lifetime of good physical and mental health.

Apart from walking, you could try any or all of the following activities:

- baseball or softball
- basketball
- biking
- bowling
- boxing
- canoeing
- dancing
- disc golf
- gardening
- golfing
- handwashing your car
- hiking
- ice skating
- jogging
- jumping on a trampoline
- jumping rope
- kayaking
- kickboxing
- lifting weights
- martial arts

- Pilates
- playing with kids or pets
- roller skating or roller blading
- skateboarding
- snow skiing
- soccer
- surfing
- swimming
- Tai Chi
- tennis
- volleyball
- water aerobics
- water skiing
- yard work

Can you commit to doing something physical every day, even if it's just going for a walk? Use the following chart to challenge yourself and keep track of your activities:

Monday

Activity: _____
Time spent: _____
How I felt afterward: _____

Tuesday

Activity: _____
Time spent: _____
How I felt afterward: _____

Wednesday

Activity: _____
Time spent: _____
How I felt afterward: _____

Thursday

Activity: _____

Time spent: _____

How I felt afterward: _____

Friday

Activity: _____

Time spent: _____

How I felt afterward: _____

Saturday

Activity: _____

Time spent: _____

How I felt afterward: _____

Sunday

Activity: _____

Time spent: _____

How I felt afterward: _____

Behavioral Activation

This activity helps with

- depression
- low motivation
- overall compassion fatigue

Behavioral activation is an exercise I often use with clients who are struggling with depression as well as compassion fatigue. When we feel down, we sometimes become caught up in a chronic cycle of both. Now, when I use the word depression, I'm referring to not only clinical depression but also certain symptoms, such as sadness; loss of interest; low motivation; sleep problems; appetite disturbances; excessive fatigue; feelings of worth-lessness, guilt, and/or hopelessness; trouble with concentration or making decisions; low self-esteem; and thoughts of suicide. Because depression robs us of our energy, we often stop doing the things that once brought us pleasure. We become less active, less social, and less motivated. As a result, we feel even more guilty or hopeless, which leads to—you guessed it—even more symptoms of depression.

By becoming more active, however, you can break this negative cycle and start feeling better about yourself. The following is a list of activities that you might find fun or relaxing and might even bring about a sense of achievement. Try to circle as many activities as you can, and feel free to add your own. I encourage you to choose at least one activity, no matter how small, every day to help you practice self-care and create more balance. You work so hard for others, and you deserve it!

take a bubble or salt bath	go to a movie
go outdoors	take a walk
read	meet new people
work on the car or motorcycle	go to the gym
go swimming	draw
have a party	go to a party
spend time with family	hang out with friends
play or learn to play an instrument	go camping
go roller skating or roller blading	color
take a drive	go skateboarding
ride a motorcycle	make a scrapbook
cook or bake	write a poem
go shopping	sew
get a haircut	go to a play
go to a concert	get a manicure or pedicure
practice photography	play with the kids
go on a picnic	go to a park
go to the beach	practice deep breathing
meditate	progressive muscle relaxation
play or snuggle with pets	go to a museum

go to an art gallery
ride a dirt bike or ATV
talk on the phone
go on vacation
listen to music
watch a comedy
play board games
go for a bike ride
take care of plants
play a sport
sing
go to a place of worship
do embroidery or cross stitch
knit
go snowboarding
get a massage
do woodworking
write in a journal
do crossword puzzles
go waterskiing
shoot pool
go snow skiing
learn a new language
practice martial arts
go to the arboretum
go to a sporting event

have coffee at a café
go bowling
take a daytrip
go on a date
go jogging
play cards
practice yoga
play video games
exercise
watch a sporting event
dance
paint
do arts and crafts
go hiking
plant or work on a garden
go out to eat
get a facial
clean or organize
do a puzzle
go surfing
relax in a hammock
go for a boat ride
go horseback riding
compose a song
go to the planetarium
go canoeing/kayaking

Add your own:

_____   _____

_____   _____

_____   _____

Behavioral Activation Journal

For each day below, choose at least one activity from your list and rate how you feel both before and after by using the following rating scale:

1—None   2—Low   3—Moderate   4—High   5—Very high

Monday   **Before**   **After**

Pleasure   _____   _____
Relaxation   _____   _____
Accomplishment   _____   _____
Depression   _____   _____
Compassion fatigue   _____   _____

Tuesday   **Before**   **After**

Pleasure   _____   _____
Relaxation   _____   _____
Accomplishment   _____   _____
Depression   _____   _____
Compassion fatigue   _____   _____

Wednesday   **Before**   **After**

Pleasure   _____   _____
Relaxation   _____   _____
Accomplishment   _____   _____
Depression   _____   _____
Compassion fatigue   _____   _____

Thursday   **Before**   **After**

Pleasure   _____   _____
Relaxation   _____   _____
Accomplishment   _____   _____
Depression   _____   _____
Compassion fatigue   _____   _____

Friday	Before	After
Pleasure	_____	_____
Relaxation	_____	_____
Accomplishment	_____	_____
Depression	_____	_____
Compassion fatigue	_____	_____

Saturday	Before	After
Pleasure	_____	_____
Relaxation	_____	_____
Accomplishment	_____	_____
Depression	_____	_____
Compassion fatigue	_____	_____

Sunday	Before	After
Pleasure	_____	_____
Relaxation	_____	_____
Accomplishment	_____	_____
Depression	_____	_____
Compassion fatigue	_____	_____

CHAPTER 6
A Healthy Attitude

*You cannot erase what you have seen once you open
your eyes to the horrors of factory farming, fur farming,
animals in entertainment, and the other animal abuses in
our world. It is both an empowering and a traumatizing
experience. The key is focusing on the empowerment.*
—MADELINE, VEGAN

Sean Davis recalls his freshman year at college being very eye opening. Davis, a shy psychology student, says that he didn't have any
interest in athletics, performing arts, or Greek life. Instead, he found
his place in the environmental and animal-rights clubs on campus. "I
remember feeling so exhilarated when I found other students with the
same passions as me," Davis says. The Mississippi native became very active
throughout the community by leafleting, protesting, and bringing awareness to social injustice. "In the beginning, I felt so energized, so hopeful,"
Davis says. "But after a while, after I became more and more aware of the
atrocities of things like factory farming and deforestation, I noticed that I
started to become angry and depressed. I started isolating myself. Even my
grades started to slip."

After taking the next summer off, he switched his major from environmental chemistry to psychology—which was a lifesaver. "I started to learn
how our emotions and behaviors are directly related to our thoughts, and

I made a real conscience effort to change my attitude," Davis says. "I also began seeing a therapist to help me process my feelings of grief surrounding the treatment of animals and the earth." He admits that it takes constant effort to keep his negative thoughts in check, but in doing so, he is able to continue his work as an animal advocate and environmentalist; he has just been accepted into graduate school with the hopes of becoming a therapist himself.

Like Davis, we all struggle with negative thinking from time to time. But when it gets to the point where our attitude begins to interfere with our work, our passions, or our life in general, then we need to take steps to change our perspective and realize that there are still good people in this world who do incredibly good things. This next chapter is dedicated to helping you change your negative or distorted thinking, cultivate gratitude, and remember the positives in your life.

Gratitude Journaling

Have you ever felt that your work with animals is a never-ending, uphill battle? Are there days when you feel like you've lost all hope for humanity? If so, you're not alone. I've known many animal caregivers and advocates who struggle to find any semblance of happiness or goodness left in the world because of what they encounter on a daily basis. The problem is that you can become so consumed with the negative side of what you do that it's difficult to remember the blessings you've been given—health, friends and family, the good people in this world, and the animals you've helped. Expressing gratitude, especially in written form, can lead to many positive benefits, including better sleep, increased optimism, improved mood (Emmons and McCollough 2003), and the ability to manage stress (Aspinwall 1998; Folkman and Moskowitz 2000). At the end of each day, take some time to jot down three things that you're grateful for. They can be as simple as a beautiful sunny day or as great as a promotion at work. Use the following worksheet or your own personal journal to give thanks on a daily basis. Remember: there is no right or wrong way to journal, it only matters that you set aside some time each day to really reflect on the good stuff.

My Gratitude Journal

Monday

1. _____

_____

2. _____

_____

3. _____

_____

Tuesday

1. _____

_____

2. _____

_____

3. _____

_____

Wednesday

1. _____

_____

2. _____

_____

3. _____

_____

Thursday

1. _____

_____

2. _____

_____

3. _____

_____

Friday

1. _____
_____

2. _____
_____

3. _____
_____

Saturday

1. _____
_____

2. _____
_____

3. _____
_____

Sunday

1. _____
_____

2. _____
_____

3. _____
_____

Positive Journaling

Whenever my sister and I spent the night at our grandparents' house as kids, I remember that my grandma would come into our room just before bedtime. She'd sit on the edge of the bed, tuck us in all nice and cozy, and ask us, "What were the three best things that happened today?"

We'd respond with answers like going swimming in the lake, brushing the dogs, or eating pizza for dinner. Maybe it was easier to focus on the good things while in the midst of childhood innocence, but in any case, somewhere along the way, I grew up and lost sight of those simple pleasures. One recent morning, however, I awoke early and decided to revel in the time I had left to stay in bed before my alarm went off. I remember feeling a gentle, cool breeze coming in from the open window and hearing the coo of a mourning dove off in the distance. It was as if the rest of the world were still asleep—no traffic, no sirens, and no barking dogs. And I just lay there, appreciating and savoring every second. For just a moment, all was right with the world.

Working in animal welfare can sometimes alter our thoughts, feelings, and overall worldview—and not necessarily in a good way. Just like with the gratitude journal, keeping a positive journal can help you remember some of the better things that happened throughout your day. So, in honor of grandma, I invite you to write down the three best things that happened to you during the day. Purchase a journal or use the following worksheet every night before you fall asleep:

Monday

1. _____
   _____
2. _____
   _____
3. _____
   _____

Tuesday

1. _____
   _____
2. _____
   _____
3. _____
   _____

Wednesday

1. _____
_____
2. _____
_____
3. _____
_____

Thursday

1. _____
_____
2. _____
_____
3. _____
_____

Friday

1. _____
_____
2. _____
_____
3. _____
_____

Saturday

1. _____
_____
2. _____
_____

3. _____
_____

Sunday

1. _____
_____

2. _____
_____

3. _____
_____

Changing Your Thinking

From the day you were born until now, you have developed certain thinking patterns. Whether they tend to lean more toward the negative or positive end of the spectrum depends on a number of factors—your temperament, how you were raised, and your overall life experiences can all influence the way you perceive and think about the world today.

Cognitive behavioral therapy, often referred to as simply CBT, is based on the theory that our thoughts—which are often automatic—lead to emotions, which subsequently lead to behaviors or consequences. For example, imagine that you look in the mirror and notice that you've gained a few pounds, you're having a bad hair day, or a brand new pimple has erupted. You think something like, "I can't go out! Everyone will notice how horrible I look!" Which *emotion* does that thought lead to? Anger, sadness, or even disgust maybe? Now, what *consequence* or *behavior* does that emotion lead to? You probably decide to stay in, miss out on the fun, and wallow in your self-hatred. But what if you put a different spin on it? What if the thought was more along the lines of, "Well, I'm sure nobody will notice, and if they do, then they probably won't care"? Now, which emotion does that lead to? Maybe you feel calm, confident, and ready to have a good time? And then, as a consequence, you go out and enjoy yourself. Notice that the exact same situation can lead to two different thoughts, which can lead to two different types of emotions, which can lead to two very different outcomes. This next section outlines the various cognitive distortions, or unhelpful thinking styles, that many of us struggle with. See if you can spot the ones that trip you up.

The Mental Filter

Imagine you work as a receptionist at a busy veterinary hospital. Many clients come and go throughout the day, some of whom you've known for years while some of them are new. You enjoy chatting with them and interacting with their pets. The end of the day is near, and you're looking forward to having dinner with some old friends. As the last client comes out of the exam room, you hand him his bill. He is clearly furious with the vet and proceeds to rant and rave that "this is a rip off" and "all you people care about is money." He slams his credit card down on the counter and continues to berate you before he finally storms out of the office, vowing never to return. Feeling angry and exhausted, you cancel your plans for the evening, opting instead to sit in front of the TV all night, dwelling on your horrible day while popping antacids.

If this type of scenario has ever happened to you, then you may have used what we mental-health professionals refer to as the mental filter. This sort of thinking style can get you into trouble because it filters out all of the positive things that happened during the day and instead allows you to focus solely on the one or two negatives. This may cause you to label situations, or even entire days, in negative terms, such as saying, "I had an awful day!" This thinking style can also cause us harm. Notice the consequences of the situation in the example: our lovely receptionist not only discounted all of the pleasant experiences she had had that day with other clients and coworkers, but she also let that one unpleasant experience spill over into her personal life by cancelling her plans and ultimately ending up with a stomach ache.

Many of us have been guilty of using this thinking style. Can you recall a time when you used your own mental filter?

Describe the situation:

_____

_____

_____

What was the thought associated with the situation?

_____

_____

_____

Was there really enough evidence to justify the thought?

_____

_____

_____

How about any evidence to contradict the thought?

_____

_____

_____

What were the consequences of the thought? (Physically, emotionally, socially, etc.)

_____

_____

_____

What would an outsider think about the situation?

_____

_____

_____

Looking at the big picture, will the situation matter in a day, a week, or a year from now?

_____

_____

_____

What would be a more helpful and positive thought in response to the situation?

_____

_____

_____

What would be the consequences of the new thought?

_____

_____

_____

Predictive Thinking

I'm sure that you've heard the phrase, "When you assume, you make an 'ass' out of 'u' and 'me.'" Well, I'm afraid this thinking style goes a bit further than that. Predictive thinking, or assuming we know what will happen in the future, can cause you a lot of heartache and stress. To illustrate, take a look at the following scenario. You're a foster parent for a local rescue group, and for months now, you've been trying to find a home for a young, playful pit bull. The past few families who have come to look at her haven't been the best fit. You have yet another meeting tonight, this one with a couple whom you're certain will not have the time nor the energy to accommodate your foster baby. You obsess all day about what a waste of time this will be and the possibility that the pooch will never find a forever home. Dinnertime rolls around, and you barely touch your food, counting down the minutes until the meeting. When the doorbell rings, you put on your best happy face and greet a young man and his new wife. The pit bull jumps onto the young woman's lap and plants a giant kiss on her face, causing the young woman to fall in love with her instantly. As you interview the couple, the man drops to his knees and begins to wrestle with the energetic pup. The couple tells you all about their new home with a large yard, surrounded by a six-foot-tall privacy fence, and how much they are looking forward to having a pet they can jog with in the morning and snuggle with at night. It turns out that you couldn't have been more wrong about the family who finally adopted the dog. Although you ended up pleasantly surprised, you'd initially let your assumptions, or predictive thinking, cause you to spend the day feeling unnecessarily frustrated and anxious.

Think about a situation in which you may have used predictive thinking and answer the following questions:

Describe the situation:

_____
_____
_____

What was the thought associated with the situation?

_____
_____
_____

Was there really enough evidence to justify the thought?

_____
_____
_____

How about any evidence to contradict the thought?

_____

_____

_____

What were the consequences of the thought? (Physically, emotionally, socially, etc.)

_____

_____

_____

What would an outsider think about the situation?

_____

_____

_____

Looking at the big picture, will the situation matter in a day, a week, or a year from now?

_____

_____

_____

What would be a more helpful and positive thought in response to the situation?

_____

_____

_____

What would be the consequences of the new thought?

_____

_____

_____

Personalization

You're a behaviorist at a local animal shelter. Part of your responsibilities includes performing temperament assessments on dogs in order to evaluate their adoptability. After working with a painfully shy shepherd mix for a few days with no success, you determine that the poor pooch isn't going to make the cut, and you mark him for euthanasia. For the remainder of the week, you can feel the cold glares and hear the whispers of some of the volunteers and staff members who had been rooting for the old dog, who had been found chained up outside of the shelter. You go home, day after day, thinking about what you could have done differently to change the canine's fate. You even start to question yourself and your right to play God at work. Your decision weighs heavily on your heart, and the week culminates with you curled up in bed crying.

Personalization is an unhelpful thinking style that can trip you up because you place an unfair amount of responsibility on your shoulders. You may take the blame for something that you have little or no control over, like the behaviorist did in the above example. Instead of looking at the external factors—the irresponsible person who abandoned the dog in the first place, the fact that the shelter was overcrowded, and the low adoption rate for senior animals— our behaviorist believed that she was completely to blame for the dog's death.

Have you ever experienced the pitfalls of personalization?

Describe the situation:

_____

_____

_____

What was the thought associated with the situation?

_____

_____

_____

Was there really enough evidence to justify the thought?

_____

_____

_____

How about any evidence to contradict the thought?

_____

_____

_____

_____

What were the consequences of the thought? (Physically, emotionally, socially, etc.)

_____

_____

_____

What would an outsider think about the situation?

_____

_____

_____

Looking at the big picture, will the situation matter in a day, a week, or a year from now?

_____

_____

_____

What would be a more helpful and positive thought in response to the situation?

_____

_____

_____

What would be the consequences of the new thought?

_____

_____

_____

Black-or-white Thinking

You're an adoption counselor at a local Humane Society. You wander outside to get a breath of fresh air, and you notice that one of your coworkers, who is also on break, is in tears. "I hate them," she sobs. "I hate everyone." The warmer weather has brought in a rash of people surrendering unwanted animals, particularly boxes full of kittens and puppies. Your once-cheerful and energetic coworker is now teetering on complete burnout. For her, the steady stream of irresponsible pet owners who had refused to spay and neuter their pets has slowly eroded her enthusiasm and energy. She now believes that humanity, as a whole, is evil. She wipes one last tear from her eye, and the two of you head back to work.

I have seen this thinking style creep up on my colleagues, and I've even experienced it myself. Working at a high-traffic shelter can cause even the best of us to become hardened and bitter, and we can begin to see things as either all good or all bad. This black-or-white thinking style leaves very little room for the gray area in between, which rationally we know exists but emotionally we sometimes lose sight of.

Can you remember a time when black-or-white thinking had a hold on you?

Describe the situation:

What was the thought associated with the situation?

Was there really enough evidence to justify the thought?

How about any evidence to contradict the thought?

What were the consequences of the thought? (Physically, emotionally, socially, etc.)

_____

_____

_____

What would an outsider think about the situation?

_____

_____

_____

Looking at the big picture, will the situation matter in a day, a week, or a year from now?

_____

_____

_____

What would be a more helpful and positive thought in response to the situation?

_____

_____

_____

What would be the consequences of the new thought?

_____

_____

_____

Catastrophizing

Fresh out of veterinary school, you land a job at a small animal hospital. One of your responsibilities is to perform euthanasia, which may involve the animals' owners being present. Your thirty-minute drive to work on your very first day is agonizing as you imagine everything that could go wrong. "What if I can't find a vein? What if the owner cries? What if *I* cry? What if I get fired?!"

As you can see, this unhelpful style of thinking is riddled with anxiety and conjures up the image of absolutely the most horrible (yet unlikely) worst-case scenario. When you get caught up in catastrophizing, your thoughts can quickly spiral out of control and cause a great deal of undue stress.

Have you ever been a victim of the catastrophe culprit?

Describe the situation:

_____

_____

_____

What was the thought associated with the situation?

_____

_____

_____

Was there really enough evidence to justify the thought?

_____

_____

_____

How about any evidence to contradict the thought?

_____

_____

_____

What were the consequences of the thought? (Physically, emotionally, socially, etc.)

_____

_____

_____

What would an outsider think about the situation?

_____

_____

_____

Looking at the big picture, will the situation matter in a day, a week, or a year from now?

_____

_____

_____

What would be a more helpful and positive thought in response to the situation?

_____

_____

_____

What would be the consequences of the new thought?

_____

_____

_____

Labeling

Another distorted thinking style comes in the form of labeling. Many of us are guilty of this from time to time, whether we apply a label to ourselves ("I feel so worthless") or to others ("People are stupid"). The trouble with this is that, for one, we're making blanket statements—no one is worthless; not all people are idiots—and two, we're ignoring everyone else's positive attributes as well as our own. The example below demonstrates how labeling can hurt all of us.

A veteran animal-control officer comes into work and discovers that he's been assigned to a certain part of town that day. "Oh, great," he says. "Another day of writing citations, catching stray dogs, and responding to countless welfare checks." The young man goes on to complain about the people who inhabit this particular part of town and how "they" can't take care of their animals. Whoa! Back up the bus. Granted, all of you ACOs do work with some "special" people out in the field, but they aren't *all* ignorant or abusive. Thinking otherwise can certainly lead to some pretty negative feelings and cause you to judge a person, or entire groups of people, unfairly.

Now, think of some labels you have used to describe yourself or others:

Describe the situation:

_____
_____
_____

What was the thought associated with the situation?

_____
_____
_____

Was there really enough evidence to justify the thought?

_____
_____
_____

How about any evidence to contradict the thought?

_____
_____
_____

What were the consequences of the thought? (Physically, emotionally, socially, an so on.)

_____
_____
_____

What would an outsider think about the situation?

_____
_____
_____

Looking at the big picture, will the situation matter in a day, a week, or a year from now?

_____

_____

_____

What would be a more helpful and positive thought in response to the situation?

_____

_____

_____

What would be the consequences of the new thought?

_____

_____

_____

Emotional Reasoning

This type of distorted thinking style occurs when we think that something is true based solely on how we feel—I feel, therefore I am. For example, have you ever been called into the boss's office and just known that you were in trouble? You have no evidence, and you can't remember doing anything wrong, yet you have this nagging feeling that you're in for it. Imagine getting yourself all worked up to the point of feeling physically ill, going into the office like a dead man walking, and then your boss tells you that you're getting a raise.

Can you remember a time when your emotions got the best of you?

Describe the situation:

_____

_____

_____

What was the thought associated with the situation?

_____

_____

_____

Was there really enough evidence to justify the thought?

_____

_____

_____

How about any evidence to contradict the thought?

_____

_____

_____

What were the consequences of the thought? (Physically, emotionally, socially, etc.)

_____

_____

_____

What would an outsider think about the situation?

_____

_____

_____

Looking at the big picture, will the situation matter in a day, a week, or a year from now?

_____

_____

_____

What would be a more helpful and positive thought in response to the situation?

_____

_____

_____

What would be the consequences of the new thought?

_____

_____

_____

Should and Should Not

Whenever we say, "I should do this" or "I shouldn't do that," we place a lot of pressure on ourselves. This type of thinking comes in handy at times: "I should probably take a walk because I just ate a giant piece of cake" or "I shouldn't speed because I might get a ticket." But this thinking style can also become unhealthy when it results in our setting unrealistic or even impossible standards. I used this one a lot in the past: "I shouldn't go on vacation because no one else can take care of my pets the way I do." Or "I can't make time for self-care because I should be out rescuing animals." Using the words "should" and "shouldn't" hurts us because we often can't live up to our own expectations, and we end up feeling guilty—even resentful—in the long run.

Do you struggle with "should" and "should not?"

Describe the situation:

_____

_____

_____

What was the thought associated with the situation?

_____

_____

_____

Was there really enough evidence to justify the thought?

_____

_____

_____

How about any evidence to contradict the thought?

_____

_____

_____

What were the consequences of the thought? (Physically, emotionally, socially, etc.)

_____

_____

_____

What would an outsider think about the situation?

_____

_____

_____

Looking at the big picture, will the situation matter in a day, a week, or a year from now?

_____

_____

_____

What would be a more helpful and positive thought in response to the situation?

_____

_____

_____

What would be the consequences of the new thought?

_____

_____

_____

Starfish Stories: The Mother of Animal Law

Joyce Tischler, cofounder of the Animal Legal Defense Fund, has always loved animals. She remembers bringing home stray kitties and injured birds when she was a child. Even when she went off to law school as an adult, Tischler continued to save animals by running a cat shelter on campus, helping hundreds of felines receive medical care and find permanent homes. Even so, there still seemed to be a disconnect with her love of animals and her dream of becoming an attorney. "There was nothing called animal law, because it had not yet been invented," says Tischler, recalling her college days in the early seventies. That all changed, however, with the publication of philosopher Pete Singer's *Animal Liberation* (1975), a highly influential book that helped launch the animal-rights movement. "Peter Singer provided me and others like me with a philosophy—animals have interests which should be protected by legal rights."

Because animal law was still in its infancy when she graduated and entered the workforce, Tischler says she didn't connect the dots between her career and her passion for animals until several years later. "In 1979, I was in private practice in the [San Francisco] Bay area and was feeling a profound disconnect," Tischler says. "I wondered how I could take my moral values about animals and apply them in my professional life." Her vision began to take shape soon after, when she met a fellow attorney who was also interested in animal rights. The two of them formed Attorneys for Animal Rights, a small group of attorneys and law students that met once a month to discuss animal-related legal issues. By 1984, the organization had grown to the national level, and the Animal Legal Defense Fund (ALDF) was born. Today, the ALDF is an internationally recognized nonprofit organization dedicated to protecting the lives of and advancing the interests of animals. The ALDF accomplishes this mission through legislative work, civil lawsuits, cruelty cases, and—most importantly—by bringing the animal-law field into the mainstream. "Most animals—by that I mean the ten billion animals annually raised in factory farms and killed for food, the millions of animals used in research and testing, those raised and killed for their fur, those who are hunted and trapped, and those exploited by the entertainment industry—are abused and exploited in myriad ways. They are powerless to stop this abuse," Tischler says. "Attorneys can help to level the playing field."

From strengthening anticruelty laws to protecting endangered species and everything in between, the ALDF has been instrumental in advancing the animal-rights movement. But even with thirty-seven years' worth of victories under her belt, Tischler isn't immune to compassion fatigue. "The most difficult part of my job is the constant onslaught of information about animals who are suffering, abused, tormented, tortured, and killed," she says. "It often feels overwhelming and never ending."

But if there's one thing nearly four decades of fighting for animals has taught Tischler, who is affectionately known as the mother of animal law, it's how to keep burnout at bay by creating a more balanced life. To recharge her batteries, as she puts it, Tischler surrounds herself with supportive family and friends—both human and animal. She reads, meditates, exercises, and enjoys live theatrical and musical events. She also nurtures her spiritual side by attending church and spending time in nature. "We are the only thing that stands between the animals and exploitation by humans," she says, "so we must try to be the best, smartest, kindest, sanest, and most effective advocates that we can be."

To learn more about the Animal Legal Defense Fund, please visit http://www.aldf.org.

Part Three

CHAPTER 7

Nourishment for the Mind, Body, and Soul

*We get our energy from what we eat, and no single
activity can change how we feel as dramatically as what
we put in our bodies each day. Nutrition is inextricably
linked to how well—or poorly—we feel and function.*
—VICKI BRETT-GACH, CERTIFIED VEGAN-
LIFESTYLE COACH, MICHIGAN

When I worked in animal welfare, I lived on a steady diet of chips, caffeinated soda pop, and ibuprofen. The caffeine kept me awake, the pain meds kept the chronic headaches at bay, and the chips, well, they just made me happy. Or so I thought. The truth is that I was a "junk-food vegan" caught up in a cycle of fueling my crappy moods with crappy food. As I learned more about veganism, I eventually began to understand not only how my diet made a positive impact on the welfare of animals as well as the planet but also how eating more fruits, veggies, whole grains, and lean proteins affected my health. I had already noticed that my annual sinus infections became a thing of the past when I gave up dairy. But when I started ditching the vending machine and eating more salads and stir fries and drinking more fresh water and fruit smoothies, I noticed that I felt better, physically and mentally.

Now, please know that I've never been the kind to push my lifestyle on others. That's not what this section of the book is intended to do. But, out of respect for some readers who do choose a vegetarian or vegan diet, we're going to focus more on a plant-based diet than anything else. Personally, I can't tell you how much of a difference it's made for me, especially when it comes to boosting my mood and immune system!

Vicki Brett-Gach, a certified vegan-lifestyle coach, explains why a healthy diet plays a crucial role in combatting compassion fatigue: "While you might be tempted to indulge in the food and drink habits that many people *associate with relaxation*, it's especially important to limit or avoid them when you're struggling with stress, depression, anxiety, low energy, and many of the other symptoms associated with compassion fatigue," Brett-Gach says. Moreover, focusing on whole, plant-based foods instead can help naturally support moods, calm cravings, and keep blood sugar levels in check. "Remember that eating well helps you be a better caregiver for others, so it's crucial to take care of *you* first," Brett-Gach says. "Make it your mission to eat well."

Food for Thought
Thank you to Vicki Brett-Gach for contributing this section.

Top Tips

- Your resilience may already be low, so be prepared when hunger strikes. Bring a small meal or hearty snack with you everywhere you go. This helps provide a little relief, whether you're at work or away from home longer than you expected.
- Go for convenience by hitting a salad bar or hot bar. You've earned it.
- Take time to create a short grocery list before you go shopping, and look for plenty of fresh foods.
- To help with digestion, take a few deep breaths to fully relax before beginning your meal.
- Drink plenty of water. Keep a refillable bottle with you, and drink plenty of pure, fresh water throughout the day to avoid even mild dehydration.

Ward off compassion fatigue by adding more of these to your diet to help nourish your mind, body, and soul:

- Sweet potatoes are high in complex carbohydrates and L-Tryptophan, an amino acid that helps prevent depression and anxiety. Because sweet potatoes are also high in Vitamin B6, they're a natural antidepressant.
- Leafy greens are among the very best foods for us on the planet; they're chock full of magnesium, iron, and B vitamins and a stellar treatment for depression. Plus, they help improve digestion and encourage healthy blood flow to the brain.
- Walnuts are another amazing food. They contain omega-3 fatty acids, which help decrease inflammation and contribute to a healthy mood. They naturally help prevent sugar cravings and induce melatonin in the body, which can help with sleep at night.
- Avocados contain high levels of folate, which can help to reduce stress and anxiety and promotes healthy brain function.
- Oats are packed with protein, magnesium, iron, potassium, and calcium that work together to promote steady energy levels in the body and reduce blood sugar and blood pressure.
- Berries are rich in phytonutrients, antioxidants, and anti-inflammatory benefits, and they can strengthen the nervous and regulatory systems. Berries are associated with a healthy metabolism, protection against cancer, and a reduced risk of heart disease.
- Hot herbal tea can be soothing, pleasantly aromatic, and deeply relaxing for those of us who suffer with symptoms of anxiety.
- Smoothies can deliver a natural mood lift, energy boost, and sense of overall well-being. Treat yourself to a freshly squeezed juice in the afternoon or check out the recipe below for a refreshing fruity green smoothie.

Fruity Green Smoothie
Serves two.

- one grapefruit, peeled and sliced in quarters
- one apple, unpeeled and cut in quarters, with the core, seeds, and stem removed
- one banana, peeled and quartered

- one to two cups of fresh baby kale or spinach
- four to eight ice cubes (optional)

Instructions

Place all ingredients in a high-powered blender. Process first on low, and then gradually work up to high speed until mixture is completely smooth. Pour into glasses and enjoy immediately. May be stored in the refrigerator for up to one day.

The list of no-nos includes the following:

- White sugar, refined flour, and highly processed foods have all been associated with symptoms of depression, anxiety, and fatigue. Refined foods can trigger an insulin spike—followed by an insulin crash. This triggers your bad mood along with the sugar cravings, both of which perpetuate the entire vicious cycle.
- Avoiding all animal products, including meat, poultry, fish, eggs, and dairy, will help you to feel more energetic and vibrant in mind, body, and spirit and improve how you feel from top to bottom, inside and out.
- Be careful with alcohol. Even occasional use of alcohol may interfere with sleep, which might already be an issue for you. If it is an issue, then be particularly cautious about having even a single glass of wine.
- Caffeine doesn't seem to affect everyone in the same way. Many people do fine with a little bit while others react with jitters, acidic stomachs, or trouble sleeping. If caffeine doesn't agree with you, then begin to cut back (if not completely quit), but do so gradually to avoid headaches.

Quick Bites

Think you're too busy to eat healthy? These wholesome snacks are perfect for people on the go. Take a few of these goodies with you to work to help sustain you both physically and mentally:

- apples
- baked tortilla chips

- bananas
- carrots
- cashews
- celery with peanut butter
- dates with almond butter
- granola or trail mix
- grapes
- hummus
- kale chips
- oranges
- pistachios
- pita bread
- pretzels
- raisins
- rice cakes
- water

Vicki Brett-Gach is a certified vegan-lifestyle coach and educator and a personal chef. For more information and delicious recipes, visit her website at http://www.annarborvegankitchen.com.

Sweet Dreams

If you've ever lain awake at night counting sheep rather than catching ZZZs, then you know how utterly frustrating it can be, not to mention how physically and mentally fatigued it can make you feel the next day. Sleep is so vital to our overall health, but according to a study by the Centers for Disease Control and Prevention, about one third of adults in the United States simply aren't getting enough (Liu et al. 2014). I can't emphasize enough how important sleep is to combatting compassion fatigue.

To help you drift off to dreamland, try the following tips:

- Establish a sleep schedule. This means going to bed at roughly the same time each night and waking up at roughly the same time each morning—even on weekends.
- Try not to take daytime naps. If you must, however, keep them short—thirty minutes or less.

- No clock watching! If you find yourself lying awake at night for more than twenty minutes, get out of bed and do something relaxing. Read a boring book, listen to calming music, or simply sit on the couch until you feel drowsy.
- Avoid alcohol, caffeine, and nicotine six hours before you snooze.
- Exercise on a regular basis, but make sure to do it several hours prior to going to sleep.
- Take a warm shower or bath before bedtime.
- Make sure that your room is suitable for slumber. Keep it cool, dark, and quiet.
- Try a sleep mask to keep out light.
- Use ear plugs, a fan, or a white noise machine.
- Turn off all electronics, including TVs, computers, and cell phones. Your brain can detect light even when you're asleep.
- Practice mindful deep breathing, progressive muscle relaxation, or guided meditation just before bedtime.
- Try one of my favorite tricks, which I call the ABC game. Pick a category—animals, vegetable, or cars—and then go through the alphabet and try to name as many things in that category as you can before you fall asleep. For example, you could list vegetables: asparagus, beets, carrots, and so on. I bet you won't make it to "z"!
- If all else fails, you may want to talk to your doctor about taking a melatonin supplement. Melatonin is a naturally occurring hormone that helps to promote sleep as well as fight depression (Uda 2016).

The Great Outdoors

In her more than fifteen years of working in animal rescue and advocacy, there have been times when Hannah Shaw has suffered from symptoms of compassion fatigue in the form of recurring nightmares, inadequate sleep, unhealthy eating habits, and a loss of balance in her life. But not today. Today, Shaw is leaving the urban chaos and never-ending demands of her job behind and hitting the trails. Shaw has made a commitment to self-care, and so she engages in regular hiking and camping and just spends some of her time in nature in order to de-stress and recharge. "In the woods, everything is how it ought to be. Every plant and every animal is free," Shaw says. "Nothing heals my heart like seeing a hawk flying free or a raccoon scurrying around in the woods." Shaw is definitely onto something, because evidence suggests that nature does indeed have a restorative effect on our well-being by combatting anxiety, depression, and fatigue; reducing stress; boosting self-esteem; and improving productivity and concentration. Studies have shown that exposure to nature increases our life satisfaction and promotes a more positive outlook (Chalquist 2009). So how can you incorporate more nature into your busy life? You don't necessarily have to travel far to reap the benefits of nature. Healing can take place almost anywhere, anytime, with a little effort and imagination.

- Take a walk outside on your lunch break.
- Go to a park, and have a picnic.
- Tend a garden—inside or out.
- Go swimming.
- Plant a tree.
- Sit quietly outside, and observe the bugs, birds, and animals.
- Go skiing or sledding during the winter months.
- Practice mindfulness, meditation, yoga, or deep breathing outdoors.
- Bring the outside in—decorate your home or workspace with elements of nature, such as rocks, wood, plants, or a small water fountain.

Mindfulness in Nature

Whether you want to escape to the dry desert, the majestic mountains, a peaceful park, or your own backyard, I encourage you to spend time outdoors and try this mindfulness activity:

- Take a moment to look around you. What do you notice? Can you see trees or water? What about animals? Without judgment, just observe everything you see.

- What do you hear? Can you hear birds chirping or leaves rustling? What about rippling water? Again, without judgment, just notice what you hear.
- What do you smell? Can you smell flowers or maybe a salty mist coming from the ocean? Without judgment, just observe.
- What do you feel? Is it raining? Is it hot and humid? Is there a chill in the air? Notice how your skin feels. Notice how your feet feel upon the earth. Without judgment, just observe.
- Use all of your senses to just observe and be in the moment.

Better Living Through Chemistry

I want to take you back in time for a moment to your high school chemistry days. Don't panic—I'll try to make this as brief and painless as possible. Let's talk about atoms and ions. You may recall that not all atoms are created equally. When the number of protons and electrons get out of whack, an atom becomes an ion. For example, when a negatively charged electron jumps ship, the atom becomes a positive ion. Likewise, when an atom picks up that electron castaway, it turns into a negative ion. What in the world does this have to do with compassion fatigue, you ask? Stay with me here. Ions, which are all around us, can have an impact on the quality of our mood and physical health. Despite their name, *negative* ions have a *positive* effect, and vice versa. OK, so how do we know whether we're being exposed to the good or bad? Have you ever noticed how refreshed you feel simply by walking along the beach or by being near a waterfall? Part of the reason is that you're being bombarded with the negative ions that are created by moving water. Pretty cool, huh?

Since the early 1930s, numerous studies have demonstrated the myriad of benefits associated with exposure to negative ions, including a decrease in depression, anxiety, and headaches, not to mention a boost in immune functioning, concentration, and energy (Lefèvre 2009). Of course, not all of us have the luxury of living by the ocean or have a rushing waterfall in our backyard. In fact, most of us live a typical twenty-first-century lifestyle that, unbeknownst to us, is chock-full of positive ions (remember, those are the icky kind). Positive ions are created by both modern-day conveniences and even nature and include electrical devices, such as air conditioners, computers, hair dryers, televisions, fluorescent lighting, air pollution, and dust. Short of giving up our cell phones and moving to a backwoods cabin, here are a few suggestions for countering the bad stuff and increasing our exposure to those oh-so-beneficial negative ions:

- Spend time in nature, especially if you're a city dweller. Head for the woods, the mountains, the water, or the country.
- Cut back on the use of electronics. Turn off the TV when you're not watching it. Ditch the dryer, and use an old-fashioned clothes line instead (your utility bill will thank you too). Speaking of dryers, let your hair air dry whenever possible. Limit your time on your cell phone, tablet, or computer.
- Take a shower. It may not compare to Niagara Falls, but the feel-good ions created by the running water can literally help you wash away stress.
- Bring plants into your home or workspace for natural protection from the pesky positive ions.
- Purchase a Himalayan salt-crystal lamp. These calming devices are made from pinkish-orange ancient sea salt and are known for generating negative ions when turned on.

Speaking of salt, I'd be remiss if I didn't mention my new love affair with this magnificent mineral. I have to confess that I've never been a huge fan of taking baths—who has the time? But that changed one night when I put my back out. I called up my sister, a massage therapist, to get some advice. Her recommendation? A salt bath. After she'd explained how salt can help the body eliminate toxins and heal achy muscles, I popped in the tub for my first—but certainly not last—salt bath. I not only felt physically better afterward, but that soak in the bath also forced me to slow down and relax. I now incorporate this practice into my own self-care routine, especially on days when I feel like I've taken in a lot of negative energy.

Healing with Salt

You can find fancy bath salts in stores or make your own at home. Here's a simple and inexpensive recipe to get your started:

1. Dissolve half a cup to one cup of course sea salt, mineral salt, or Himalayan salt into a warm bath.
2. Add fifteen to twenty drops of lavender essential oil. (You can find essential oils at many health food stores or online.)
3. Soak for ten to twenty minutes.
4. Drink plenty of water afterward to rehydrate.

Don't always have time for a bath? Try this relaxing shower scrub! Combine the following into a container:

- one cup fine sea salt
- half a cup oil (coconut, almond, jojoba, grapeseed)
- five drops lavender essential oil
- three drops peppermint essential oil (optional)

Top Tip

- Be careful when using the scrub in the shower, and always stand on a nonslip bath mat. The oil in this recipe can make your skin oh-so-soft, but it can also make your tub oh-so-slippery!
- If you have ultra-sensitive skin, you may want to substitute sugar in your scrub.

The Healing Arts

As I mentioned earlier, compassion fatigue is not a black-and-white issue. In my experience, it's something that ebbs and flows in terms of severity. There have been particular times in my life when compassion fatigue has existed quietly in the background and other times when it has been at the forefront and downright debilitating. I remember one such time when I really struggled with intrusive thoughts and nightmares after learning about dairy production and its connection to the veal industry. As you may or may not know, calves are torn from their mothers at birth—traumatizing them both—and then the males, who are useless to the dairy industry, are tied up, confined to tiny crates, and kept in the dark. Since the animal is not allowed to exercise, let alone turn around, its muscles are not able to develop properly. This practice, in addition to keeping the calf malnourished to produce anemia, is done intentionally to produce tender meat.

After reading about and watching undercover videos of the veal industry, I felt extremely hopeless, depressed, and traumatized. But there were two things I did to help myself feel more empowered. First, I gave up dairy. Second, I wrote a song about it. It's called "In the Dark" and tells the story of what I imagine it feels like to be a calf taken from its mother, put in a veal crate, and eventually slaughtered. If you're interested, you can find it at a variety of online stores, including iTunes and Google Play.

As a drummer and composer, writing or playing my instrument has always been cathartic for me. There are times when I believe that music has saved my life. But you don't have to be a trained musician or songwriter to reap the benefits of music—or any other art form, for that matter. Research suggests that incorporating artistic expression in our lives—whether through our own creations or by appreciating others' creative endeavors—can have a positive impact on our psychological and physical well-being (Staricoff and Loppert 2003).

While artistic expression is limited only by your imagination, I've highlighted a few ideas as follows to get your creative juices flowing.

Expressive Writing

Expressive writing involves putting difficult thoughts and feelings to paper. Writing about a stressful or traumatic incident has been suggested as a way to help people process and assign meaning to negative experiences, as well as learn how to express their emotions in a healthy way. Dr. James W. Pennebaker, who has conducted extensive research on the benefits expressive writing, notes that while the technique can help a variety of people, it may be especially helpful for men who tend to suppress their emotions (2014).

In their book *Expressive Writing: Words that Heal* (2014), Pennebaker and coauthor Dr. John Evans explain the myriad of health benefits associated with expressive writing:

- It helps to regulate emotions (Petrie et al. 2004).
- It reduces stress by lowering blood pressure and heart rate (Pennebaker et al. 1987).

- It decreases rumination as well as symptoms of anxiety and depression (Lepore 1997).
- It helps to relieve anger.

Since all of the techniques that these authors recommend are beyond the scope of this book, you may want to try your hand at expressive writing by using the following exercise:

- Commit to writing for at least twenty minutes for a minimum of four days in a row.
- Start by writing about what's bothering you the most, but feel free to switch to other emotionally charged topics if that's where your writing takes you.
- Write about a stressful or traumatic event that you're currently experiencing and that's having a negative impact in your life right now.
- Keep in mind that feelings of sadness are common immediately after you complete the exercise, so allow yourself some time to process what you've written.

Please note that, depending on the severity of the trauma, you may want to wait several days or even weeks to start the writing process. If the incident is still fresh, then you may not be ready to address the painful emotions—*and that's OK*. Write only when you feel ready.

Coloring

The popularity of adult coloring books has been on the rise, and although it may seem like just another trend, therapeutic coloring can be traced back to the early twentieth century. Psychiatrist Carl Jung was known to use mandalas, which are circular symbols that originated in India, as a way to help his clients reduce stress (Santos 2014).

Although research on the benefits of adult coloring is still in its infancy, many therapists I have talked to can provide anecdotal evidence on the calming effects that the activity has on clients. Some suggest that coloring brings us back to the innocence of our childhoods. Others propose that by focusing on coloring mandalas, which are symmetrical and repetitive by design, people tend to let go of distressing thoughts and emotions. This type of structured coloring helps people decrease their anxiety by putting them into a meditative state (Curry et al. 2005). And the best part about adult coloring books? You don't have to be an artist to create beautiful artwork. Plus, it's a relatively inexpensive and portable hobby. Pack a coloring book and a box of colored pencils, and get creative—and de-stress—on your lunch break.

If you want to give coloring a try, start by downloading some free coloring sheets at my website, http://deepwatermichigan.com. Need some more ideas? Check out these artistic endeavors that you can do to cultivate creativity and combat compassion fatigue:

- Make a collage.
- Start a scrapbook.
- Go dancing.
- Write a poem.
- Sew.
- Try a new recipe.
- Watch a play, musical, ballet, or opera.
- Go to a concert.
- Create homemade pet treats or toys.
- Draw or paint.
- Compose a song.
- Write a story.
- Go to an art gallery.
- Make jewelry.
- Do woodworking or metalworking.
- Join a band.
- Practice photography.
- Build a sandcastle.
- Build a snowman.
- Learn to play an instrument.
- Make homemade soap or candles.
- Take up knitting, cross-stitching, or crocheting.
- Listen to music.

- Do arts and crafts.
- Get involved with community theater.
- Learn to sing.
- Add your own ideas:

_____

_____

Want to take the creative challenge to see if it makes a difference in your mood? Use the following worksheet, and notice what makes you feel better:

Monday

Activity: _____
Time spent: _____
How I felt afterward: _____

Tuesday

Activity: _____
Time spent: _____
How I felt afterward: _____

Wednesday

Activity: _____
Time spent: _____
How I felt afterward: _____

Thursday

Activity: _____
Time spent: _____
How I felt afterward: _____

Friday

Activity: _____
Time spent: _____
How I felt afterward: _____

Saturday

Activity: _____
Time spent: _____
How I felt afterward: _____

Sunday

Activity: _____
Time spent: _____
How I felt afterward: _____

CHAPTER 8

Protecting Yourself: Boundaries, Communication, and Taking a Social-Media Vacation

> *I try not to think about what [animals] have been*
> *through, because the stories you do know about are*
> *the stories that most people couldn't even imagine.*
> —COURTNEY, ANIMAL RESCUER, COLORADO

very animal welfare warrior needs protection before going off to battle. But we're involved in a different kind of war—the kind where tanks and bulletproof vests do us little good. The kind of protection we're going to explore in this next chapter has to do with the ways in which we can shield ourselves mentally and emotionally to avoid succumbing to the wounds of compassion fatigue and burnout. We're going to talk about what personal boundaries look like and how you can work to set more healthy ones. We'll look at different types of communication styles and how they can either help or hurt you. And finally, we'll discuss the role of social media in animal welfare today, and I'll explain the importance of taking a break from the Internet from time to time.

Setting Healthy Boundaries

In Robert Frost's "Mending Wall" (1914), his neighbor insists that, "Good fences make good neighbors." What I take from that proverbial expression is that we all need personal barriers, or boundaries, to keep us safe.

Boundaries take many forms: they can be physical, sexual, intellectual, spiritual, material, temporal, emotional, and so on. But unlike property lines, personal and professional boundaries can sometimes be hard to define, especially in an emotionally charged caregiving field like animal welfare. What do boundaries look like? Let's explore three types.

Rigid Boundaries

If our personal boundaries are too rigid, like the stone wall between Frost and his neighbor, then we may find ourselves feeling lonely, detached, and isolated. Our walls become so thick and inflexible that we distance ourselves from others, sometimes even the ones who we love the most. Instead of protecting us, our rigid boundaries end up hurting us.

Loose Boundaries

Of course, if we tore that wall down completely, then that would leave us pretty vulnerable, just as loose or porous boundaries might. If you tend to have loose boundaries, then you might struggle with saying no. You might find yourself becoming overly dependent on others, oversharing personal or inappropriate information, or allowing others to take advantage of or even abuse you.

Healthy Boundaries

Somewhere in the middle of having a stone wall and no barrier at all is a nice chain-link or wooden privacy fence. Healthy boundaries are not so permeable as to deprive us of any protection, yet they are not so impenetrable as to keep the entire world out. When we have healthy boundaries, we value the opinions of others while still respecting our own. We're clear and confident about our own wants, needs, and personal limitations—and this means knowing when to say no. Healthy boundaries not only promote self-respect, but they also foster healthy relationships and make us better caregivers. Although setting healthy boundaries takes practice and may seem a bit awkward at first, remember that these boundaries are building blocks to a solid foundation that supports personal, professional, and compassion satisfaction.

Assertive Communication

One way to cultivate healthy boundaries is to practice being assertive. We all have our own unique way of communicating with others based on how we were raised, the relationships we've had, and our life experiences in general. But just like with boundaries, there are healthy and not-so-healthy ways of communicating. Take a look at the following communication styles and place a mark next to the characteristics that apply to you. Keep in mind that you probably interact differently in various situations, so think of how you behave with others as it relates to your work with animals.

Passive Communication

_____ I am too quiet and/or have a hard time standing up for myself.

_____ I often find myself avoiding eye contact or looking down when confronted.

_____ I tend to be a "people pleaser" and have a hard time saying no.

_____ I usually put my own needs last.

_____ I allow others to ignore, bully, or abuse me.

_____ I frequently apologize to others even if they are at fault.

Aggressive Communication

_____ I often use a loud, angry, or threatening tone of voice.

_____ I have become physically violent or abusive with others.

_____ I often find myself using aggressive body language, such as intense eye contact, clenching my fists, or invading others' personal space.

_____ I usually put my own needs first.

_____ I am frequently argumentative, angry, sarcastic, or disrespectful toward others.

_____ I find myself pushing my own wants, needs, beliefs, or values on others.

Assertive Communication

____ I am able to verbalize my own needs while respecting others.

____ I treat other people with respect.

____ My body language is relaxed with appropriate eye contact.

____ I know how to compromise and say no when appropriate.

____ My tone of voice is polite and respectful, and I listen to others.

____ I can stand up for myself if I feel that I'm being taken advantage of, bullied, ignored, abused, or otherwise being treated inappropriately.

Assertiveness Training 101

- Use a relaxed tone of voice that is neither too quiet nor too loud to express your needs.
- Keep your head held high, and maintain good eye contact.
- Try using "I" statements like, "I feel angry," or "I feel _____ when you _____ because _____." rather than "You always piss me off!"
- Use the reflection technique to mirror what the other person is saying or feeling. For instance, "It sounds like you feel..." or "So what you're saying is..."
- Avoid using criticism, poor judgment, profanity, defensiveness, name-calling, and sarcasm.
- Refrain from using words like "always" and "never" as they tend to make people defensive.
- Be sure to listen to others without interrupting them, and be respectful of their opinions.
- Stand up for your own rights, and know when to say no.
- Know that changing your communication style won't happen overnight. Start small and practice, practice, practice!

Now, let's explore how your own boundaries and communication styles may impact you.

Can you think of any situations that make you feel taken advantage of, unappreciated, or even abused? _____

_____

_____

Are there times when you let someone else's opinions, beliefs, or values override your own? _____

_____

_____

Are there times when you ignore your own needs to the point of feeling exhausted or resentful?

_____

_____

_____

When it comes to your role in animal welfare, what type of boundaries do you have?

_____

_____

_____

How did your immediate family, your culture, or larger society help to define your current boundaries?

_____

_____

_____

How do your current boundaries help?

_____

_____

_____

How do they hurt?

_____

_____

_____

What will life look like if you don't create healthy boundaries?

_____

_____

_____

What will life look like if you _do_ work to set healthy boundaries?

_____

_____

_____

What steps are you willing to take to create healthy boundaries?

_____

_____

_____

What type of communication style best describes you?

_____

_____

_____

How did your immediate family, your culture, or larger society help to develop your current communication style?

_____

_____

_____

How does your current communication style help?

_____

_____

_____

How does it hurt?

_____

_____

_____

What will life look like if you don't learn assertive communication?

_____

_____

_____

What will life look like if you *do* learn assertive communication?

_____

_____

_____

What steps are you willing to take to develop assertive communication?

_____

_____

_____

Taking a Break from Social Media

Not a day goes by when I don't have petitions waiting for me in my inbox or grizzly photos and videos of animal abuse popping up on my Facebook page. When I first became involved with animal rights, the Internet had yet to be invented (can you imagine!). I learned all that I could about the movement from other living, breathing humans as well as from books. When the World Wide Web was born, I had all the world's knowledge at my fingertips, and with the click of a mouse, I was able to educate myself on animal issues through undercover videos, graphic images, and gruesome testimony. I became obsessed—and traumatized. And the more traumatized I felt, the more I felt compelled to educate myself so that I could do all I could to prevent animal suffering. It became a vicious cycle.

It took me a long time to realize that, after a while, I wasn't educating myself anymore; I was tormenting myself. I strongly believe that one of the keys to keeping compassion fatigue at a minimum is to cut back on the use of social media. I'm not saying that you should go so far as to be ignorant of what's happening in the world, but it's important to protect yourself. My motto is, be informed enough to get fired up but not so informed that you burn out. These days, I set aside specific times to focus on signing petitions, and I limit my exposure to violence in the media. I also try to be mindful of what I post on social media to avoid traumatizing others. And I really make it a point to watch all those heartwarming or humorous animal videos that make their way around cyberspace because watching them helps to balance me emotionally. Most importantly, I no longer feel guilty for taking a break from social media when I need to. After all, what is the point of having all that knowledge if you don't have the energy to act on it?

CHAPTER 9
Finding Support

*I would say that the biggest tip is just knowing that we
need to take care of ourselves in order to best help others.
We are better advocates and activists when we aren't
exhausted and depressed, but when we are energized.*
—MELANIE JOHNSON, ANIMAL ACTIVIST
HELPLINE COUNSELOR

Let's face it, folks: life can be tough. Especially when you care so much that it hurts, as Dr. Bev Heater so eloquently said in the beginning of this book. So what if you've done all that you can with this workbook but still need more? Research has shown that, in addition to implementing a self-care regimen, obtaining support is another crucial piece of the puzzle when it comes to managing compassion fatigue. Whether it's a trustworthy friend or coworker, a pastoral counselor, a licensed mental-health profes- sional, or even an online support group, having people to confide in can make all the difference in the world.

Individual Therapy

Deciding to seek the help of a therapist is a very brave thing to do and, in my opinion, a true sign of strength. It's not easy to sit down with a com- plete stranger and talk about your innermost thoughts, desires, hopes, and dreams—let alone secrets, fears, and neuroses. But what we know about therapy is that the very act of talking about your problems actually creates new neural networks—that's basically psycho-speak for healing the brain (La Rose 2015). And you know what? Even therapists seek therapy from time to time! But how do you go about finding a mental-health professional who can understand the unique challenges that those of you in the animal-welfare community face? My advice would be to find someone who specializes in compassion fatigue, trauma, or grief and loss. These folks may be better equipped to handle the graphic stories that you may want to share. Does your organization have an employee-assistance program? If so, then check out the resources they offer. If not, then why not advocate for getting one started?

When it comes to getting professional support, I wouldn't worry too much about a therapist's theoretical background (psychodynamic, cognitive behavioral, and so on). Research tells us that the key to successful therapy is less about technique and more about the relationship between you and your therapist (Meyers 2014). So how do you know if you and your therapist are a good fit?

Top Ten Tips to Find a Great Therapist

1. Your therapist should be warm, empathic, and nonjudgmental. If you feel that your therapist judges you or your lifestyle, then this is a huge red flag. Your therapist doesn't necessarily have to share your beliefs or values, but she should accept and respect them. If you're a vegetarian and your therapist tries to convince you to eat meat, or if you're struggling with pet loss and your therapist dismisses your grief, then find another therapist!

2. Your therapist should not dispense unsolicited advice or make decisions for you; rather, he should act as a collaborator to help you gain your own insights and come to your own conclusions. While making suggestions such as, "You many want to consider taking long walks to help lift your mood, because research has shown..." are appropriate, your therapist should never tell you what to do based solely on his own opinion—for example, "I think you should leave your husband. I would never put up with a cheater."

3. Your therapist should be nice. This should be a given, but would you believe that I've had several clients thank me for not yelling at them? Your therapist should always treat you with a warm, positive regard. If instead he gets frustrated or angry with you, disrespects you, blames you, or talks down to you, then this is a clear sign that the therapist has his own unresolved issues and is taking them out on you.

4. Your therapist should be able to handle whatever you throw at her. One of the most valuable things I learned in grad school is that you can only take your clients as far as you've gone yourself. Your therapist should know what it feels like to be the client and should have worked through her own issues. If you find that your therapist gets squeamish or changes the subject when you bring up certain topics, then these could be signs that she's uncomfortable—and, ethically, she has a responsibility to refer you to someone else.

5. Your therapist is not your friend. While you should feel comfortable and safe with your therapist, it is his responsibility to uphold certain professional boundaries. Your therapist should not meet with you casually outside of sessions, engage in an intimate relationship with you, or force upon you unwanted attention, such as hugging you, touching you, or otherwise invading your personal space.

6. Your therapist should be more interested in your problems than her own. While some self-disclosure on your therapist's part is OK if it enhances the therapeutic relationship or process, your therapist should never talk incessantly about herself, rely on you to console her, or try to force you to follow her agenda.

7. Your therapist should be professional. He works for you. This means that he should show up on time and be fully present during your appointment. He should not eat in front of you, nod off when you're talking, or answer the phone during sessions.

8. Your therapist's job is to eventually work herself out of a job. While some people require or even enjoy long-term therapy, others benefit from short-term support. Some of the goals of therapy are to help you develop new coping skills and a healthy support system outside of therapy. Your therapist's focus needs to be on helping you get better, not keeping you indefinitely to fulfill her own financial needs.

9. Your therapist must be sensitive to your race, religion, ethnicity, sexual orientation, and so on. We live in a very diverse, multicultural society, and while therapists can't be expected to be experts on every single culture, they should be respectful to and comfortable with people from all walks of life.

10. Your therapist should not only be a good listener, but he should also be able to help you gain personal insight, develop healthy coping skills, change unhelpful thinking styles and behaviors, establish healthy boundaries, strengthen relationships, and attain overall personal growth and happiness with your life.

Where Can I Find a Therapist?

- Ask trusted friends, family members, or colleagues if they know a therapist they would recommend.
- Get a referral from your doctor or insurance company. Be advised that not all insurance companies will cover therapy without a mental-illness diagnosis, and if there is a diagnosis, keep in mind that this can stay on your permanent record! For these reasons, plus the ability to ensure confidentiality, some therapists are private pay only.
- Check out the following online directories:
  - www.pychologytoday.com
  - www.goodtherapy.org
  - www.theravive.com
  - www.therapistlocator.net
  - www.networktherapy.com
  - www.openpathcollective.com
  - www.vegan-therapist.com
  - www.onlinecounselling.com

Support Groups

In addition to or instead of individual therapy, you may find comfort with some of the following useful support groups.

Animal Activist Online Support Group

This is a free online support group that focuses on compassion fatigue and other issues that those in the animal-welfare community face. Presented by In Defense of Animals, an international organization dedicated to animal rights and rescue, this confidential group meets on the fourth Thursday of each month from 5:00 to 6:00 p.m. PST. Register at http://www.idausa.org/campaigns/council-sustainable-activism/upcoming-events/.

Compassion Fatigue in Animal Shelter/Rescue Workers

This Facebook group, dedicated to animal-advocacy professionals, offers information on compassion fatigue and online support. Check it out at https://www.facebook.com/groups/9231699886/.

Pet Loss/Anticipatory Bereavement Chat Rooms

Offered by the Association for Pet Loss and Bereavement, these free online chat rooms offer support to anyone who has lost or is anticipating the loss of a companion animal. Please visit them at http://www.aplb.org.

The Grief Support Center

This website provides a variety of chat rooms, including one for teens only, for owners of pets with cancer, the Monday Night Candle Ceremony, and general pet-related grief. For more, visit http://www.rainbowsbridge.com.

The Pet Loss Support Page

The Pet Loss Support Page offers a directory for finding local support groups and therapists, tips on coping with grief, and more. Check it out at http://www.pet-loss.net.

Grief Support Chat Room

Find support and advice through online chat rooms, candle ceremonies, poetry, and more at http://www.petloss.com.

Wrong Side of the Rainbow Discussion Group

This Facebook group offers support and information on both compassion fatigue and pet loss grief. Join at https://www.facebook.com/groups/532572386793162/.

Hotlines
United States

In Defense of Animals Animal Activist Helpline:
1.800.705.0425 or helpline@idausa.org

National Suicide Prevention Lifeline:
1.800.273.8255

ASPCA National Pet Loss Hotline:
1.877.GRIEF-10

Canada

Suicide Hotline:
1.800.SUICIDE

Pet Loss Support Hotline:
519.824.4120, ext. 53694

Great Britain

Society for Companion Animal Studies Support Line:
0800 096 6606

Creating a Supportive Work Environment

Nothing can fuel the flames of compassion fatigue and lead to burnout faster than a toxic work environment, as we learned in chapter two. If you're a director, manager, owner, or supervisor, then this section may be especially helpful to you.

Education

- Boost awareness of compassion fatigue. Many employees may feel alone in their struggles. Becoming educated about compassion fatigue and normalizing the accompanying feelings can help staff members feel less isolated and better equipped to handle the stress that comes with animal-welfare work.
- Team up with a specialist or mental-health professional to offer workshops on compassion fatigue, grief, stress reduction, anger management, and other pertinent topics.
- Encourage professional development by offering free training, paid time off for conferences, and/or financial assistance with continuing-education classes.
- Consider cross-training your staff so that, for example, the same person isn't stuck performing euthanasia all the time.

Self-Care

- Create a wellness-friendly atmosphere by allowing—and insisting—employees take breaks, including for lunch. Suggest that they get outside the building to take a walk or practice relaxation exercises.
- Offer workplace benefits that foster self-care, such as gym memberships or massage gift certificates.
- Install a vending machine or stock the company fridge with healthy snacks and plenty of water. Be sure to include vegan and gluten-free options.

Environment

- Make the break room a haven for employees and volunteers. Consider adding soft lighting, soothing colors, plants, and a self-care board that staff members can post positive messages on—or their favorite ways to tackle compassion fatigue.
- If possible, set aside space for employees to use for yoga, meditation, or relaxation exercises during their breaks.

- Have policies in place—and enforce them—to prevent workplace gossip, bullying, blame, and harassment. We're all in this together.
- If euthanasia is part of the job, then help out your staff by creating a room that reflects calm and comfort rather than a prison cell. Use soft lighting, paint colors, and music. Always have staff members work in pairs, and place all techs on a rotating schedule. Never euthanize animals in front of other animals.

Staff Input

- Have a suggestion box for employees and/or volunteers to contribute to. Consider having a contest, such as suggestion of the month, and give out prizes that encourage self-care—like an extra day off.
- Give staff members a say. Allow for flexibility in their work schedules, and accommodate for sick days and vacations.
- Create opportunities for team members to discuss stressful, challenging, or traumatic situations by holding regular debriefing sessions during which they have a safe, supportive, and confidential space to express themselves. You don't have to be a trained expert to facilitate these meetings—just listen and validate.

CHAPTER 10

Your Toolbox

*Self-care is so important. You cannot
serve from an empty vessel.*
—ELEANOR BROWNN

Now that you've completed the workbook, you've had a chance to try some, if not all, of the activities. Now it's time to build your own personal toolbox. What works for you? What do you want to learn more about? What are you willing to commit to? Keep in mind that, according to experts, it takes at least two months to break old habits and cultivate new ones (Grohol 2009), so don't beat yourself up if you don't notice any immediate changes. Instead, make it your personal mission to take baby steps every day by using your new-found tools. Remember, you can't go to the gym once and expect to build muscle or lose weight. It takes time, effort, and commitment to combat compassion fatigue.

Try to answer the following questions to help you build your toolbox.

What stands out the most for you from this workbook?

_____

_____

_____

What have you learned about yourself as you've worked through the book?

_____

_____

_____

_____

What will life look like if you make a concerted effort to manage compassion fatigue?

_____

_____

_____

What will life look like if you _don't_ make any changes?

_____

_____

_____

What changes would you like to make in the next year?

_____

_____

_____

What steps can you take in the next three months to help you reach those goals?

_____

_____

_____

What baby steps can you take today or in the coming week to contribute to your goals?

_____

_____

_____

What would you like to learn more about?

_____

_____

_____

What is the most difficult part of your job or role in animal welfare?

_____

_____

_____

What is the most rewarding?

_____

_____

_____

What tools do you want to utilize when you're feeling particularly vulnerable to compassion fatigue? Please check all that apply to you right now, but feel free to revise as needed.

_____ mindfulness

_____ deep breathing

_____ progressive muscle relaxation

_____ guided meditation

_____ massage therapy

_____ anger management

_____ walking or other exercises

_____ yoga

_____ behavioral activation

_____ getting more negative ions

_____ taking salt baths or showers

_____ gratitude journaling

_____ positive journaling

_____ changing thinking styles

_____ getting creative

_____ joining a support group

_____ individual therapy

_____ working on personal boundaries

_____ working on communication styles

___ developing healthy sleep habits
___ improving diet
___ spending time in nature
___ cutting back on social media
___other: _____

Starfish Stories: My Story

REFERENCES

American Institute of Stress. 2012. "Take a Deep Breath." *Daily Life Blog.* http://www.stress.org/take-a-deep-breath/.

American Pet Products Association. 2016. "Pet Industry Market Size & Ownership Statistics." http://www.americanpetproducts.org/press_industrytrends.asp.

American Medical Veterinary Association. 2016. "Human-Animal Bond." https://www.avma.org/kb/resources/reference/human-animal-bond/pages/human-animal-bond-avma.aspx.

Anxiety and Depression Association of America. 2014. "Exercise for Stress and Anxiety." http://www.adaa.org/living-with-anxiety/managing-anxiety/exercise-stress-and-anxiety.

Aron, E. 1996. *The Highly Sensitive Person.* New York: Broadway Books.

Aspinwall, L.G. 1998. "Rethinking the Role of Positive Affect in Self-regulation. *Motivation and Emotion* 22:1–32.

Ayl, K. 2013. *When Helping Hurts: Compassion Fatigue in the Veterinary Profession.* Lakewood, CO: American Animal Hospital Association Press.

Baranowsky, A. and E. Gentry. 2010. *Compassion Fatigue Specialist Training Workbook.* Traumatology Institute.

Bushman, B.J. 2013. "Anger Management: What Works and What Doesn't." https://www.psychologytoday.com/blog/get-psyched/201309/anger-management-what-works-and-what-doesnt.

Chalquist, C. 2009. *Ecotherapy: Healing with Nature in Mind.* San Francisco: Sierra Club Books.

Corliss, J. 2015. "Mindfulness Mediation Helps Fight Insomnia, Improves Sleep." *Harvard Health Blog*. http://www.health.harvard.edu/blog/mindfulness-meditation-helps-fight-insomnia-improves-sleep-201502187726.

Doige, N. 2015. *The Brain's Way of Healing: Remarkable Discoveries and Recoveries from the Frontiers of Neuroplasticity*. New York: Penguin Books.

Dolce, J. 2013. "Interview with Patricia Smith: Founder of the Compassion Fatigue Awareness Project." *Notes from a Dog Walker (blog)*. https://notes-fromadogwalker.com/2013/09/12/patricia-smith-compassion-fatigue-awareness-project/.

Emmons, R.A., and M.E. McCullough. 2003. "Counting Blessings Versus Burdens: An Experimental Investigation of Gratitude and Subjective Well-Being in Daily Life." *Journal of Personality and Social Psychology* 84 (2):377–389. doi:10.1037/0022-3514.84.2.377.

Etzion, D. 1984. "Moderating Effect of Social Support on the Stress-burnout Relationships. *Journal of Applied Psychology* 69 (4):615–622.

Figley, C. 1995). *Compassion Fatigue: Coping with Secondary Traumatic Stress Disorder in Those Who Treat the Traumatized*. New York: Brunner/Mazel.

———. "Traumatization and Comfort: Close Relationships May Be Hazardous to Your Health." (keynote presentation at the Families and Close Relationships: Individuals in Social Interaction Conference, Texas Tech University, Lubbock, TX, February 1982.

———. 2012. *When Helping Hurts: Preventing and Treating Compassion Fatigue*. http://www.giftfromwithin.org/html/PTSD-Videos.html.

Filen, S.L., and R.H. Llewellyn-Jones. 2006. "Animal-Assisted Therapy for Dementia: A Review of the Literature." *International Psychogeriatrics*. 18(4): 597–611.

Folkman, S., and J.T. Moskowitz. 2000. "Positive Affect and the Other Side of Coping." *American Psychologist* 55:647–654.

Froeliger, B., E.L. Garland, and F.J. McClernon. 2012. "Yoga Meditation Practitioners Exhibit Greater Gray Matter Volume and Fewer Reported Cognitive Failures: Results of a Preliminary Voxel-based Morphometric Analysis." *Evidence-Based Complementary and Alternative Medicine* 2012. doi: 10.1155/2012/821307.

Frost, Robert. 1914. *North of Boston.* Academy of American Poets. https://www.poets.org/poetsorg/poem/mending-wall.

Geisler, A.M. 2004. "Companion Animals in Palliative Care: Stories from the Bedside." *American Journal of Hospice and Palliative Care* 21(4): 285–8.

Grohol, J. 2009. "Need to Form a New Habit? 66 Days." Psych Central (blog). http://psychcentral.com/blog/archives/2009/10/07/need-to-form-a-new-habit-66-days/.

Ikram, S. 2005. *Divine Creatures: Animal Mummies in Ancient Egypt.* New York: American University of Cairo Press.

Jessen, J., F. Cardiello, and M. M. Baun. 1996. "Avian Companionship in alleviation of depression, loneliness, and low morale of older adults in skilled rehabilitation units." *Psychological Reports* 78(1): 339–48.

Kabat-Zinn, J. 1994. *Wherever You Go, There You Are: Mindfulness Meditation in Everyday Life.* New York: Hyperion.

Killian, K. D. 2008. "Helping till it hurts? A multimethod study of compassion fatigue, burnout, and self-care in clinicians working with trauma survivors." *Traumatology* 14: 32. doi: 10.1177/1534765608319083.

Kraybill, O. G. 2015. "Neuroplasticity 101 for Trauma Survivors." Psych Central (blog). http://pro.psychcentral.com/neuroplasticity-101-for-trauma-survivors/008247.html.

Kubler-Ross, E. 1969. *On Death and Dying.* New York: Macmillan.

La Rose, L. 2015. "More Than Just Talk—How Psychotherapy Changes Your Brain. http://www.theravive.com/today/post/More-Than-Just-Talk-How-Psychotherapy-Changes-Your-Brain-0001750.aspx.

Larkin, M. 2015. "Study: 1 in 6 Veterinarians Have Considered Suicide." *Journal of the American Veterinary Association.* https://www.avma.org/News/JAVMANews/Pages/150401d.aspx.

Lefèvre, C. 2009. *Himalayan Salt Crystal Lamps: For Healing, Harmony, and Purification.* Toronto: Healing Arts Press.

Libby, D. J., F. Reddy, C. E. Pilver, and R. A. Desai. 2012. "The Use of Yoga in Specialized VA PTSD Treatment Programs." *International Journal of Yoga Therapy* 22. http://www.veteransyogaproject.org/uploads/6/4/4/5/6445971/ijyt_article.pdf.

Liu, Y., A. G. Wheaton, D. P. Chapman, T. J. Cunningham, H. Lu, and J. B. Croft. 2014. "Prevalence of Healthy Sleep Duration Among Adults—United States." *Morbidity and Mortality Weekly Report (MMWR)* 65:137.

Mayo Clinic. 2016. "Yoga: Fight Stress and Find Serenity." http://www.mayoclinic.org/healthy-lifestyle/stress-management/in-depth/yoga/art-20044733.

Meyers, L. 2014. "Connecting with Clients." *Counseling Today.* http://ct.counseling.org/2014/08/connecting-with-clients/.

National Institutes of Health. 2009. "Can Pets Help Keep You Healthy? Exploring the Human-Animal Bond." *NIH News in Health.* http://news-inhealth.nih.gov/2009/February.

Oren, G. K. 2013. *Yoga: The Trainer's Inside Guide to Your Workout.* Heatherton: Hinkler Books.

Reeve, C. L., S. G. Rogelberg, C. Spitzmüller, and N. DiGiacomo. 2005. "The Caring-Killing Paradox: Euthanasia-related Strain Among Animal Shelter Workers." *Journal of Applied Social Psychology* 35:119–143.

Rhoades, R. 2001. "Sentence for Salvation." *ASPCA Animal Watch.* https://www. petfinder.com/animal-shelters-and-rescues/volunteering-with-dogs/ prison-dog-programs/.

Ross, C. B. and J. Baren-Sorenson. 2007. *Pet Loss and Human Emotion: A Guide to Recovery.* New York: Routledge.

Sharma, A., V. Madaan, and F. D. Petty. 2006. "Exercise for Mental Health." *Primary Care Companion to the Journal of Clinical Psychiatry* 8 (2):106. http://www.ncbi.nlm.nih.gov/pmc/articles/PMC1470658/.

Siegel, D. J. 2010. *Mindsight: The New Science of Personal Transformation.* New York: Bantam Books.

Singer, P. 1975. *Animal Liberation.* New York: Harper Collins.

Stamm, B. 2009–2012. "Professional Quality of Life: Compassion Satisfaction and Fatigue Version 5 (ProQOL)." ProQOL.org. http://www.proqol.org/ uploads/ProQOL_5_English_Self-Score_3-2012.pdf.

The Compassion Fatigue Awareness Project. 2013. "What is Compassion Fatigue?" http://www.compassionfatigue.org/pages/compassionfa-tigue.html.

Tiesman, H. M., S. Konda, D. Hartley, C. C. Menéndez, M. Ridenour, and S. Hendricks. 2015. "Suicide in US Workplaces, 2003–2010." *American Journal of Preventative Medicine* 48 (6):674–682. http://www.ajpmon-line.org/article/S0749-3797(14)00722-3/fulltext.

Time. 2014. "Seven Ways Pets Improve Your Health." http://time.com/94581/7-ways-pets-improve-your-health/.

Tremayne, J. 2010. "UK Suicide Study Prompts Call to Act." *Veterinary Practice News.* http://www.veterinarypracticenews.com/May-2010/U.K.-Suicide-Study-Prompts-Calls-To-Act/.

Uda, Rachel. 2016. "A Multitasking Molecule." *Psychology Today Magazine*, March/April, 31.

Vormbrock, J. K., and J. M. Grossberg. 1988. "Cardiovascular Effects of Human-Pet Dog Interactions." *Journal of Behavioral Medicine* 11 (5):509–17. http://www.ncbi.nlm.nih.gov/pubmed/3236382.

Williams, S. 2016. "Director of Taiwanese Animal Shelter Commits Suicide After 'Feeling Distraught About Having to Euthanize Too Many Dogs.'" *Daily Mail.* http://www.dailymail.co.uk/news/peoplesdaily/article-3604719/Director-Taiwanese-animal-shelter-commits-suicide-feeling-distraught-having-euthanise-dogs.html.

Wolkin, J. 2015. "How the Brain Changes When You Meditate." http://www.mindful.org/how-the-brain-changes-when-you-meditate/.

About the Author

Jennifer Blough is a professional counselor, certified compassion-fatigue specialist, certified pet-loss grief recovery specialist, and the owner of Deepwater Counseling in southeast Michigan. She provides individual, couples, and group counseling and offers compassion-fatigue workshops and retreats for animal-care professionals. She shares her home with her husband and their eight rescue babies: three dogs, two rabbits, two mice, and one parrot.

You can reach Jennifer at jennifer@deepwatermichigan.com. Sign up for her e-newsletter to receive additional resources, including helpful articles, self-care tips, relaxation tools, news on upcoming events, freebies, and other goodies at www.deepwatermichigan.com.

Index

Made in the USA
Middletown, DE
20 December 2018